D0849957

Crisis in Watertown

Crisis in Watertown

The Polarization of an
American Community

by Lynn Eden

Ann Arbor—The University of Michigan Press

Copyright © by The University of Michigan 1972
All rights reserved
ISBN 0-472-29875-5
Library of Congress Catalog Card No. 77-185150
Published in the United States of America by
The University of Michigan Press and simultaneously
in Don Mills, Canada, by Longman Canada Limited
Manufactured in the United States of America

To my parents

Acknowledgments

My first and greatest debt is to the people of Watertown; I thank them for sharing a small period of their existence with me, and for their great kindness. I would like to thank Alan Kromholz for his patience and cooperation, and Kathy and Frank Isaacson for providing me with friendship and a much-needed sense of home during the summer of 1970.

The Residential College community of the University of Michigan has been supportive in many ways. The college allowed me the freedom to research and write this as part of my undergraduate education; I cannot possibly express my gratitude to the community for the richness of my experience there. The Urban Studies Concentration program of the Residential College very helpfully granted me a stipend from the National Science Foundation Undergraduate Research Participation Program. Max Heirich, Alfred Meyer, Theodore Newcomb, and Marilynn Rosenthal have all given me very important encouragement, intellectual stimulation, and criticism. Nancy Aries, Judith Guskin, and Jody Sims have critically and very helpfully read the first draft. Marilyn Young's comments on that draft were especially helpful.

Several discussions with my parents were important, as was their support throughout.

Finally, to William Porter, who guided me through all stages of the writing so patiently and with great insight, a special thanks.

Contents

And you shall know the truth,
and the truth shall make you free.

JOHN 8:32

On May 19

On May 19, 1968, the minister of the Congregational Church of Watertown, Wisconsin, was fired. He was fired by a divided congregation; the vote was 133 to 77. The minister, Alan Kromholz, had an undeniably powerful presence and spoke with conviction of the new world to come, a world that would be brought about by non-violent revolutionary change. Kromholz believed it imperative that this country, and the world, undergo far-reaching social change, and that it is the role of the church to participate in this social transformation. However, the majority of his congregation believed that "a minister has to decide in this day and age whether he's going to play the politics game or the religion game. . . . They don't mix."

The crisis in Watertown went beyond a conflict concerning the definition of the church, although that was an important and integral issue. The crisis was rather one of confrontation with the prospect of radical social change — radical, that is, in the context of Watertown. That this confrontation was not unique but a manifestation of underlying tensions in the nation was the intuition that brought me to Watertown in the summer of 1970, between my junior and senior years in college. I lived in town for two months and, tape recorder over my shoulder, talked with people about the firing, about themselves, and about the world in general.

The East Side Bakery, Marge and Joe's World Bar, gas stations, the L and L Luncheonette, a large dandelioned field bordered by "the wall" where teenagers sit — these are the elements of Watertown's Main Street. The sidewalk is studded with cast iron planters, nine feet off the ground so children and animals won't tear out the petunias. And on the corner of Sixth and Main, a peculiarly American constellation: a green popcorn stand, a Bell Telephone booth, a mail box, and on the side of the Hotel Washington, a sign painted in red and yellow, "Chinese Food."

The town spreads out from Main Street, the yellow brick houses lying under a vast canopy of maples and elms, the Rock River running in a wide arc through town. Somewhere on the outskirts, in the area that is not quite town or country, lie factories.

Looming above Watertown are the church spires, the tallest structures in town, and although they take second place to the business institutions as the lifeblood of the community, they have an important social role in Watertown, and for many, a spiritual one as well. Although it is not the most imposing structure, the Congregational Church is considered by many Protestants to be "the best" church in town. In 1967 the congregation had over four hundred and fifty members, including the then Mayor of Watertown, the Chief of Police, several city aldermen, and a number of very prominent businessmen. It was this church that was the locus of conflict. More than ten years ago the Congregational Church merged nationally with the Evangelical and Reformed Church, which is of similar congregational structure and of primarily German background. The merger, the United

Church of Christ, has a national leadership that is considered, at the least, to be progressive. The complete title of the local congregation, the First Congregational United Church of Christ, is cumbersome and the church is generally referred to as the Congregational Church or the U.C.C.

In 1967–68, when this drama took place, Watertown had a population of approximately fifteen thousand. Over a hundred years ago, because of a large German influx, it was the second largest city in Wisconsin. The visitor to Watertown today senses the pervasiveness of German background through names: family funeral homes named Schmutzler, babysitters named Baumann, dachshunds named Hans. At one time there was a significant Irish population and I was told that the Irish and Germans used to throw each other into the Rock River in fierce battle. There is no such animosity now. There are a few Mexican-Americans in the area, largely because of a migrant camp several miles outside of town. There is one black family in Watertown, an elderly couple whose children have grown up and moved away.

Watertown is not isolated physically or economically. Nine miles off I-94, it lies almost directly between Madison to the west and Milwaukee to the east. It is an hour's drive to Madison and just a little more to downtown Milwaukee. Watertown has local industry with national markets, G. B. Lewis Company, Durant Manufacturing Company, Brandt Automatic Cashier Company, Watertown Table Slide Corporation, and several local branches of national industries. The importance of industry to Watertown is best told by the town itself. The introduction to its Chamber of Commerce booklet, "A Good Place to Live," reads:

Watertown — a city of promotion-minded retailers. Watertown — a small but thriving industrial complex. Watertown — a good place to work and play. . . .

Recent remodeling of many of Watertown's retail businesses has shown the desire of local merchants to serve the

40,000 area residents that comprise the Watertown marketing area.

A monthly farmer's market festively reminds the people of Watertown of the rich farming area that surrounds the community.

But it is the trains and trucks heading for Milwaukee and Chicago that are the barometers of Watertown's main strength — industry.

A wide variety of consumer and industrial products are manufactured by local companies that have found Watertown an excellent location for their operations. Continual plant expansion of many of these industries provides evidence of their successes.

This is Watertown, our town. A good place to live, work, and play.

We like it here.

The drama that was enacted in Watertown was set not only in place but in time. Throughout 1967 the war in Vietnam escalated. In March of that year troop strength in Vietnam was approximately 425,000. In May the U.S. Commander in Vietnam, General William Westmoreland, urged a further buildup of American troops. The summer of 1967 saw the largest urban riots in the history of this nation, among them Newark, Detroit, Minneapolis, Milwaukee; Plainfield, New Jersey; Hartford, Connecticut; Kansas City, Missouri; Waterloo, Iowa; Cambridge, Maryland. In August President Johnson announced that U.S. forces in Vietnam would be increased to 525,000 by June 1968.

The year 1968 was a time of presidential primaries, and of murder. On March 31 President Johnson announced to a surprised nation that he would not seek re-election. On April 4 Dr. Martin Luther King, Jr., was assassinated. Shortly after, in response to the assassination, a federal fair housing act was passed, one that would not go fully into effect until 1970. On April 11, the same day the papers carried the story about the federal legislation, Secretary of Defense Clark Clifford announced a call-up of reserves for active duty in Vietnam and set a new troop ceiling of 549,000. On June 5 Senator Robert Kennedy was fatally shot. And although we did not know it then, the massacre of My Lai had taken place on March 16 of that year.

Two years later, the summer of 1970, saw the invasion of Cambodia and the fatal shootings of students at Kent State University and Jackson State College.

This then is the context in which a minister in a small town was fired and in which subsequent conversations concerning that firing took place.

II

I spoke with Oscar Schmutzler, Sr., a white-haired man in his seventies, in the reception room of the Schmutzler Funeral Home. His first reaction was, "Oh, I didn't expect you to be so young. You're not a beatnik, are you?" I assured him I was not. He adjusted his hearing aid; it shrieked, then quieted, and we began.

"Pertaining to Reverend Kromholz, he made one mistake," Schmutzler said. "See, you have to understand the nature of the community here. He just didn't fit in. All he was interested in was civil rights. You have to understand the nature of the races. You see, the Negroes are the most different from our race. Of all the races, they are the most different from ours. They're very high-strung. I think you'll agree with me on that. And when they get a little, they want more. They're not relaxed. Now the yellow race, they're more like we are — more — submissive. When the Negroes got their civil rights they wanted more. Now, some of them are highly cultured, I'm not saying they're not. No doubt about it. They have lawyers and doctors but the vast majority, well, when this civil rights law was passed, when? four or five years ago, and then many of them came up from down South and they weren't prepared. They just didn't fit in."

Because of a lack of education?

"Well, yes, because of a lack of education, and ability. Now that isn't to say that's true for all of them. For example, in town we have a very nice Negro family, the

Goodies. 'Course it's only the old couple left now but when their sons were growing up, they were just fine children — in the band, on the baseball team, just fine children.

"Now the thing about Reverend Kromholz. You see, it's going to take a long time for this to change. Generations. Generations. You can't just change so fast. It will take three or four generations to change the Negroes. They want to change it too fast. It takes people a long time to accept the changes and what Reverend Kromholz wanted to do was change it too fast. And what Reverend Kromholz did was to undermine the authority of parents in the community. He just didn't agree with our ways and then he took some of the kids into Milwaukee marching with — what's his name? Oh, Father Groppi, and then the kids came back and told their parents all sorts of things that their parents didn't agree with.

"For the first six months he seemed all right. See, Alan Kromholz told us he was an activist and that's all right, that was okay with us so long as he was an activist — the right way. And kids are activists too, that's why he could influence them so easily. Reverend Kromholz didn't act his age at all. He was — twenty-nine I believe."

And he acted younger, or what?

"Oh yes, much younger," Schmutzler said. "You see, he wouldn't cooperate with us. He was too extreme, too obstinate. We called this meeting to discuss this with him but he said he just couldn't change his views, and wouldn't. And just wouldn't cooperate with us and so we couldn't have him. He just didn't agree with our ways and where would this country be if authority breaks down?"

Was that the main problem, that he was corrupting the youth? I asked.

"Yes," Oscar Schmutzler said. "Yes, that's it exactly. What I want to emphasize is the difference between Reverend Kromholz and the rest of the community. He just didn't fit. He was too extreme. And so he couldn't stay."

Alan Kromholz was twenty-nine when he came to Watertown with his wife, Ruth, and two small boys. Kromholz began his ministerial duties in February 1967, fifteen months before he was dismissed. He is a pleasant-looking man of medium build, with brown hair that is slightly receding and unusually blue eyes. He speaks with assurance.

"To live to the full potential that I'm creative, I have to act," Kromholz said.

What had he expected?

"I expected from my parish just the opportunity to be priest and prophet. And to be accepted as both. My purpose was simply to bring people to an awareness of the condition of their community, to bring their Christian witness to bear on the problems of that community, and to change it. To make Christianity alive.

"The community was dead. The kids were dead. There was no hope, no one was thinking, no one was being creative, no one planning, everyone was just existing, whether it was the principal of the school, or the school board, or whatever it was. Well, the system was dead and this in itself required action. And that's practically what the parish had said to me when they called me to their church. We want someone who is involved in social action, someone who can turn on young people. We want new thought, new blood, new programs, new ideas. And if all they wanted was, heh, someone who could *tell* them about these programs or someone who could point to the literature about involvement and sit back and wait till they had enough faith in their leadership to try it, they were mistaken. They didn't say that. They wanted leadership, and that's what I tried to provide.

"The whole process was one of making them aware, getting them involved, of bringing them to the point of *acting*, because in acting they would at least be giving some answers, putting meat at least on the bones of the answers that they believed should be there."

Alan Kromholz told me that when he was in Watertown he saw the church as a center for revolutionary change. He said during the more agrarian period of the country the church had made a significant ministry but with "the industrialization of communities the church became, in my opinion, nothing but a projector of the *image* of culture. It no longer ministered to the needs, it no longer led people.

"It was my feeling that if the church could once again begin to minister to the needs of man, the church could once again become a viable force. All right. Therefore to do this task, to minister to the needs of the people, to the needs of mankind today, the church would have to take on a revolutionary structure and it would have to make the determination that it would not simply mouth platitudes but that it would commit itself to action, that it would very clearly know what those goals of action were, such as political involvement, such as organizing to develop the kinds of ordinances within a city, for fair housing for example, that would not only provide equal opportunity, that would not only give justice to people, but would educate the children that it was bringing up. Bring them to the point of understanding that this is how men must live and act today. Okay, that's the revolutionary church."

I said that perhaps the needs he saw for the congregation were not the needs they saw for themselves.

"That is very possible," Kromholz said. "And I think that might be true, except that I would say that the prophetic church, which is going to stand as the center of revolution, which has a theology of involvement with mankind, or the world, to bring about the kingdom of God, the situation of peace and brotherly love, demands that we not simply look at the parish, or the members of the church and confirm their navel-gazing.

"Certainly the men and women of the parish have needs and they must communicate those needs. But they must communicate them in theological terms or language, and they must also evaluate their needs under the light of theology, what the church really demands. And they must understand what the church, Christianity, or Judaism, is all about. And the fact [is] that we have, I believe, theologically illiterate people in the church who have no understanding of the God-man relationship.

"Let's take the whole concept of the Bible. That God demands from man a response that is one of stewardship for people and things. And that's that each man build up his brother and not seek a protection of self or a false security. And if the church is going to accept the fact that the needs of the church, or the needs of the parish, or the needs of the people are determined by their own decision that they need peace, and they need peace in the manner of, for example, having a war in Vietnam, then that's false. That's false theology. That's contrary to the church and really, they are not Christian.

"I don't accept the fact that you determine or I determine what my needs are as a Christian and therefore demand that the church meet my needs. That's really what I meant when I said that the church simply mouthed culture. We mouthed imperialism, we mouthed capitalism. And we asked the church to support that, and the church did. So long as it stood on the side and prayed for people marching to war and for power for the Commander in Chief of the armed forces, in a sense what it was doing by that action, that conservative action, was supporting the conservative position. It was allying its power, and the church does have power, with the conservative imperialism. I don't think the church, if I look at it from the way I've just tried to project it, is ever neutral.

"Certainly when I was called to Watertown I believe that I was called to be more than simply a spiritual voice to administer the sacrament and to meet that very human need of counseling and of ministering to the sick and the dying and the bereaved. I was called as a priest-prophet. That's my understanding and I certainly tried to make that very clear to the group that called me, to the committee, that I was to stand as a witness and as a voice in that community. And in some way that's what I hope was projected in my ministry in terms of what was demanded of the people, that they were to be prophetic voices, witnesses."

Alan Kromholz grew up in the small town of Merrill, Wisconsin, which he said was almost brick for brick like Watertown's Main Street and bakeries. He told me that certain things about small towns are fact, such as the provincialism, the bigotry, and the industrial problems "where the laboring classes were really truly exploited by the owners of industry."

Kromholz was brought up in a home of strong German discipline. His father was president of the Boot and Shoe Workers' local and a fiercely independent and conservative Republican. His mother at one time was party chairman for the Republican Party in Lincoln County and Kromholz had been the organizer for the Republican Party during his junior and senior years at Elmhurst College. He said he was a staunch supporter of Nixon, even in 1960 when he ran for office against Kennedy. Kromholz said he was attacked by a number of theological professors in seminary which caused him less to reflect than to try to undergird his Republicanism. In early 1960 he joined a group called Four Freedoms, which he said was like the John Birch Society.

Kromholz described it as "a conservative, rather fascist kind of organization. I attended some of their meetings, went to some of their study groups with some other seminarians. And in that process couldn't stomach some of the things that were said, some of the attitudes and some of the actions. I was the only one who would raise questions at meetings about the tapes we would listen to. Why did an individual say [what he did]? What was the background? That we didn't know any kind of thing about the individual or the tape, that we were being fed propaganda, let's think. And got slowly turned off by the group.

"And then went overseas in 1962, and I would say that's when my transformation began. Began at Drew University. I met a man by the name of Doctor Monlonday who was a U.N. diplomat, became the president of the United Front for the Liberation of Mozambique, was leaving this country to go back and head that movement, was assassinated a year ago now. Monlonday was a product of our mission schools, became a great diplomat, and then went back to lead the revolutionary movement.

"I went to Chile. I saw poverty, was engaged with people, certainly felt their tremendous struggle. Saw the great economic power of Anaconda Copper, up on a hill above a village that was — dying. Thirty-three percent of the people were unemployed — great sickness, no medical facilities.

"Came back to this country and still I had questions about the civil rights movement, but then went South."

Kromholz told about his experience in the South to an interdenominational women's group in May 1967, and according to the Chief of Police he also told this story at a seminar held in September at which the Chief was speaker. When I asked him to repeat the story Kromholz said, "In '64, in May, sometime between the first and the tenth of May, I went to Canton, Mississippi, with ten other men from Eden Seminary, to work in voter registration — and to be part of some non-violent confrontation or dialogue with the white community in Canton.

"We went down, we participated in voter registration, we met the normal types of harassment, being stopped by police at night with the flashing of spotlights in your eyes, being detained by a squad car pulling up in front of you and not allowing you to cross the highway, having police surveillance, which I very stupidly thought in the beginning was for our protection.

"On Wednesday night I think it was some of us went downtown to Canton with the express purpose of eating at a white restaurant and having dialogue with the members of the white restaurant about the problems of racism in the South and why blacks couldn't, for example, get into the show, why they couldn't get into the local Farmers' Home Administration and make applications for loans to bring their rural living quarters up to minimum conditions, and to talk about the church's and northern Christians' concepts of involvement. And that evening we were beautifully served in that restaurant. I think we had southern fried chicken, and we had a great kind of dialogue among ourselves. But no one talked with us.

"So there were six of us who decided the next morning we would go back and have breakfast in the restaurant and once again try to have some dialogue or make a presence of white community. And we had been sitting in the restaurant for about forty-five minutes in the morning to get waited on and at one point, I believe before we were waited on, a guy came from the back of the restaurant, and it was evident that he had been somewhat disturbed earlier, and basically he came up to us and said, 'What the hell you doing down here?' which shook us a little bit, a confrontation of that nature. But we said, well, we were down here to witness for our faith, to be part of a movement for racial justice. And at that point I had moved my hands from under the table to above the table, and the guy made some comment about, 'Don't move.' So I had somewhat of a personal encounter with this guy simply by moving my hands. And his comment then was, 'You know there's gonna be a hell of a lot of trouble.'

"This was our fourth or fifth day in Mississippi and we decided that when a guy we would say was a redneck would say that, that we'd better put some stock in it, and we would leave the restaurant. So our breakfast came, we believed they were giving us a hard time, and we rather hurriedly ate that and then left. We paid our bill and walked out one by one and that was I think where we made somewhat of a mistake. Well, I had walked out onto the street. I was the fifth of six."

Was it a deliberate strategy to walk out one by one?

"Oh no. Normally don't you just pay your bill and walk out? Well, even though we were somewhat upset by this guy, we weren't so upset to say, 'Well, now we must immediately take precautions.'

"So as I walked out onto the sidewalk, there was a police officer sitting in the squad car right across the street. If I had walked across at the cross walk to the other side I could have shaken his hand. He was sitting in a squad car and the redneck who had made the encounter in the restaurant came out of the drugstore right next to the restaurant and as I walked out, grabbed me and pushed me up on the hood of a car. So as the guy pushed me up on the top of the car he said again basically, 'What the hell you doing here?' and I didn't answer, slid off the hood of the car, and then between two cars which were angle parked on the street. So he grabbed hold of me and began slapping me, open handed, which wasn't too bad, and then he stopped and he turned to me and he said, 'God damn you, ain't you going to fight?' And my reaction was simply to relax and put my hands at my side. Why, I don't know, this was just fact. I knew I wasn't going to confront him.

"Well, by this time there's a crowd of people coming down the street and converging. This is on Main Street, there's a police car across the street, and as I looked this guy in the eye, after he said, 'God damn, ain't you going to fight?' well, he slugged me and knocked me down in between these two cars. By that time the group of men I had been with had backed the car we were in down the street and had the door open. So I was laying in the street between two cars and just crawled over and got in the back seat, that seat lay forward and I just crawled in the back, and we took off.

"Well during that entire encounter the officer didn't come over and say, 'Hey fellas, let's knock off the fighting.' He *sat* there in his car. He was still there when we left.

"So all right, in the process I got my teeth chipped. Okay, that's fine. It was at that point that I began to truly believe some of the things about police brutality that were said. Later that day some men from the Justice Department, Attorney General's office came to investigate the situation and so I explained what had happened and basically their comment was, 'Well you realize that every minister who would come down here would have to be beaten and slapped around and have his teeth chipped and then we could show intent to deny your civil rights. So it happened to one out of four hundred. We can't show any intent. There's nothing demonic about this. There's really nothing you can do.' It was at this point that I began to question 'justice' a little bit too. Unless you want to make a charge against the individual with the local police, and should they track him down, and should they be able to find a jury, and should they in the South then determine that he's guilty, all of these things, then of course there will be some justice."

By 1964 Alan Kromholz was certainly voting Democratic, and "felt that we have to have some form of revolutionary change. Not violent. Non-violent revolutionary change."

I asked him how he would describe America today.

"It's a capitalistic society," he said. "A *strong* capitalistic society. The poor are always going to be abused, as long as we have the system of taxation that we have, the system of management that we have. And the charity of capitalism is not going to produce the kinds of medical-social support programs that is now required by America as it becomes part of the twenty-first century. We are a country of great industry, production, but we no longer are in an age of industrial society. That's not the goal and the objective of the country any longer. The goal must become one of — if industry, capitalism and the movements to mass production et cetera dehumanize man, now we must be in a period of really — rehumanizing man and bring to bear the benefits of society, the benefits of really a humanity that provides medical services for example for the elderly, for the sick, that has the kind of mental attitude that will take care of the man, the woman, who does not want to work, who opts not to work. We've got to turn the resources of society around and I think that will happen only under a form of socialistic state where we direct resources for all of the citizens of the country rather than towards an accrual of capital by the leaders of the five hundred industrial firms of the country."

How do you see America's relation to the rest of the world?

"I don't think America's relationship or attitudes or objectives in relationship to the rest of the world has changed at all during the 1900's. Or take the late 1880's to today. We are still an imperialistic nation. We carry the flag with us. We no longer seek to establish ourselves as a super power but to underscore the fact that we're a super power. That we are the maker of treaties and control the economic policies of the world. We are a consumer of raw materials and that is the kind of situation we are quite happy to keep somewhat in balance. And that's not changed over probably the last one hundred years. I think the world, particularly the Third World, really correctly sees us as an imperialistic nation. We've never propagated concepts of really — liberalism to the world. We've become a super power and we're very happy."

I V

Weir and Vivian McQuoid, a couple in their forties, were among the very staunchest of Alan Kromholz's supporters.

Mrs. McQuoid is a librarian at the junior high school and McQuoid, whom everyone calls Mac, is the wrestling coach at the high school. The first night I met them, Mac discussed the feasibility of flying his flag upside down as a sign of distress over U.S. involvement in Cambodia. He would have liked to but then would have had to stay home from school to defend it. He was sure someone would take it down otherwise. Mac told me that frankly he's a very successful coach and very secure in his job, but politically he's left and they just can't figure that out. "Of course," he said, "I'm not so far left as they think."

I started out with some very broad questions such as what they thought was most important in what happened, what was their direct involvement, and their relationship to the Kromholzes.

Vivian McQuoid said, "I don't have too much to say."

"First of all," Mac said, "I was on the pastoral committee that chose Al. I was one of two people who made the suggestion that the church employ him. The other was Myrl Pauli [the church secretary]. I think our involvement with Al came about first with church camping, and [I] saw in him a rather unique, different kind of a concerned pastor. I knew him two years before. In fact, one year we lived in the same cabin together and when you live and rub shoulders, you get to know a person pretty well, and I think there is where we developed a sense of feeling for one another. While I never was I guess you could say, as radical as Al was, there was never any question in my mind that what he was doing was right for him and in return he never felt that he should try to greatly influence my life because what I was doing was right for me. And I think that this spirit of camaraderie that developed out of this relationship you don't get with very many people in this world.

"We thought that he would be good for this community if they would be willing to accept him. It ended up, of course as you know, they didn't accept him very well. I don't think this church is really ready for involvement. In anything. I think they don't mind *hearing* liberal or even radical statements as long as the person speaking does not *do* what he's saying. And I think this is basically true for anyone in the community who *acts* rather than just talks."

Vivian McQuoid said, "It was a case of the whole community was involved after awhile. It wasn't just our church. It seemed that the whole city was involved in this, because our people didn't keep it to themselves. They just talked. Rightly or wrongly they were talking and they were bringing in everybody."

Mac said that Kromholz's one fault was that "people either became so intensely involved with him that they were *all* for him or that they were so intensely opposed to him that they would have nothing to do with him. I think he tried to polarize people but then he had no way of bringing about reconciliation, and this was his greatest fault. I think that he was so intent upon change that really the result of the conflict that was created was not of any real concern of his.

"I think that his wife was considerably different. I think that his wife recognized what he was doing much better than he did, in relationships. Ruth's role was that of the compromiser. Throughout the period she could still talk to people. People would say to her, so sorry you're going, after he got fired. But they wouldn't say anything about her husband. Ruth bore the brunt of frustration. She received the hate phone calls because Al was so often out. She was the compromiser and bearer of the cross. We sort of protected Ruth. If we knew Al would be gone for the day, even on legitimate church business, we'd just say, come on over, and that way she wouldn't have to be at home to get any kind of calls."

Mac said, "He influenced me, but he influenced me the most by influencing my children. I think he took me into the depths of real — religion. And he did it by influencing the kids, the girls, and then the girls would come home and we would sit and talk this out. A big influence on me was that Sydney [the McQuoids' daughter] was ostracized. People polarized us together as a family. Her hate phone calls were my hate phone calls. Since then, it's been my family first, the church second, and work third. Before, my work was first. I think it was *the* period in our lives that most greatly changed our total family relationship."

First Tensions

I

The beginning of Alan Kromholz's ministry, like most ministries, was not exceptional. I was told that he was personable; the church's monthly publication, the *Church Chimes*, shows that he tried to visit every home in the congregation but did not succeed. It was not until the end of the summer that small tensions, such as a hospital call he failed to make during his first week in Watertown and an insert in the church bulletin that some felt was political in nature, began to be seen as manifestations of larger issues.

The summer of 1967 was the summer that urban riots tore the country. Most important to those in Watertown, it was the summer that Milwaukee rioted.

On August 28, after Mrs. Vel Phillips, Milwaukee's only black alderwoman, had been defeated four times in introducing an open housing bill in Milwaukee, Father James Groppi, white advisor of the NAACP Youth Council in Milwaukee, launched a campaign to pass open housing legislation in the city. The effect of Father Groppi's marches on those who lived in Watertown, an hour's drive from Milwaukee, was great.

Public Opinion: Father Groppi

"The thing that irritates me is that he was *marching,* and that destruction was happening because he was marching. Maybe he has drawn more attention to the problem, I don't know. But I can't approve of that way of getting at the problem. Through marching. Gosh, everybody's got something they'd like to have, well suppose everybody goes out and—everything's relative. If they were using some of their time that they're marching, they're wasting their shoe leather and they're really not *learning* anything. If they wanted to learn I would think they'd best spend their time in some kind of a training program."

Peg Buckland

"Just to watch him on TV was enough to make you sick. I would swear he was so — ill. Just the way he talks. Whether he incited them [the riots], I don't know. I think he whipped up some — don't you think anybody who has a good speaking way about him or something, they know the right words and at the right time, can do a lot of damage? I think he did. He felt their plight I suppose and he felt justified. When you listened to him talk and his eyes would just glow when he was talking about his mother. I kinda wonder about his background, if there wasn't something — neurotic about him somewhere. [laughing] He would wave his arms and oh, I can't explain but I actually had a dislike for him, poor guy."

Jean Bertling

"I couldn't say that I knew him as a person except that I've met him on occasions. And I think that Jim did more for Milwaukee than Milwaukee will ever realize. I think that a lot of the things that are happening there, they would not have got down to the nitty gritty unless Jim's marching with his kids, or something similar, had happened, see. Now I realize that this is the kind of thing that makes people lots of enemies right away see. I realize that, but I think nevertheless in a place like Milwaukee it *had* to happen in order to get the thing — Jim I think is his own worst publicity agent. . . . I admire him very much, I think he's a very good priest, I think he's in love with God and his fellow man, and [laughing] I send him some money once in awhile."

Father Vincent Thilman

"I'll tell you, frankly, I've always been a very strong supporter of Father Groppi, but there again, honey, he's made mistakes. Well, there again there's only been one perfect man and that was Jesus. Not Moses, Paul, any of them. And Father Groppi made mistakes. But at the same time, I consider the good he did overshadows that. In other words, we're not supposed to be perfect. He had to be beautiful. He did it from the heart."

Walt Goodie

"To my way of thinking Father Groppi is a very serious criminal who is teaching crime to a lot of unhappy and neglected people, and people who are willing to accept a false doctrine."

Bernard Traeger

"In this town they think Groppi's crazy. Place I worked at, very conservative people who've lived in Watertown all their lives, 'Well, what's Groppi doing tonight?' They laughed it off. They'd say, 'What's he doing marching all these people around? People in Milwaukee I've talked to, the same thing. They never understood *why*. If they're so worried about poverty, why don't they go out and get a job? People just don't understand."

Michael Bausch

Father Groppi's marches lasted for months and attracted national attention. At times, over one thousand people marched. Father Groppi and the Youth Council, and also the Committee for Racial Justice of the United Church of Christ, along with other denominations, sent out a call to pastors from across the country to come to Milwaukee to assist in the struggle for open housing.

Alan Kromholz was among those who went. When I asked him how he came to march with Groppi his immediate response was, "How did I come to march with Groppi? Groppi was marching." That summer Kromholz had been elected state chairman of the Commission on Social Concerns of the United Church of Christ and in that capacity was involved in mobilizing clergy and public opinion. "I was involved in that and it seemed therefore natural, being involved in the mobilization, that one would get involved himself. And I did," he said. Kromholz marched with Groppi several times, as did Weir McQuoid and a few teens in the congregation. This caused conflict in some families where the parents were opposed to their children marching.

II

Mike Bentzin was mayor of Watertown during Alan Kromholz's tenure and is a member of the Congregational Church. Bentzin is a large man in his later sixties, tanned and vigorous, and speaks in a deep voice. He grew up in Watertown and after playing professional football in the newly formed National League for one year (and once having his jaw thrown out for two weeks by Jim Thorpe), came back to run the family grocery store. He has long been active in civic affairs and besides being mayor for two years, was president of the Police and Fire Commission for ten, and was on the Vocational School Board and the Watertown School Board for a number of years. Until very recently he had not been on any church boards. "I never was the type of fellow to be on a church board," Bentzin said, "and I didn't have the time with all the other."

The first time I talked with Mike Bentzin he asked me where I was from.

Detroit, I replied.

"No, I mean your parents or grandparents," he said.

Oh. My grandparents are from Russia. All of them.

Bentzin, knowing that I had spent some time in Watertown previously, then asked, "Have you been to church here?"

No, no I haven't.

"Never?"

Well, I was only here for a very short time. I paused. Besides, I'm Jewish.

"Oh," said Bentzin, "that's what I meant."

He then asked if I thought I could understand a church conflict and I told him I thought I could, that we fire our rabbis too.

A little later he asked me if I was in SDS. I told him I was not.

The Bentzins' home is tastefully furnished. Mike Bentzin showed me with some pride the large pieces of petrified wood he and his wife had carried back from Wyoming, where one of their sons lives, and the glazed brick that covers a large middle strip of their patio. He told me he grabbed the brick a few years back when the city tore down part of Main Street. His wife, Joy, collects annual Scandinavian Christmas plates, a different design every year, and has a collection of Royal Copenhagen and of Bing and Grondahl dating back some fifteen or twenty years.

Their cars have bumper stickers on them in red, white, and blue that say, "Combat Communism. Support Our Troops in Vietnam."

Discussing Kromholz, Bentzin said, "See, the first six months his sermons were good, just fine. I had done some checking on him in Evansville, I was on the road for a food broker three days a week and this store was right near the church he used to be at. So I asked about him and they said, 'You can have him!' He had brought a Negro family in from Madison to live there and there wasn't any reason for it and finally they just moved out again. So they told me he'd been monkeying around and brought this colored family in and that we sure could have him, that he was just a troublemaker.

"And he seemed okay for about six months, nice

sermons, young fellow, but then the minute Father Groppi got marching, all of a sudden he was off like that." Bentzin snapped his fingers.

"Must have been biding his time. The Chief checked on him in Milwaukee. He was there with Groppi. Holy minnie, they were out there marching. And he took those *kids* into Milwaukee to march. Let Milwaukee solve their problems and Watertown theirs. You take a fellow like Kromholz who's actually dangerous. They're leading our young people to not listen to their parents, to not go to church."

Was this the most dangerous thing about him?

"Well, yes, except if he'd kept going into Milwaukee. They were hauling food in there and what all. They should have kept it themselves. And they had people up here, prostitutes, car thieves." Referring to Barbara Williamson, a secretary of Father Groppi who spoke at a church-sponsored seminar in September 1967, Bentzin said, "This gal, Barbara Williamson, her folks were reliable colored people. He worked for the city I think. He [Kromholz] had all sorts of car thieves up here talking to our young." Bentzin showed me a two-page report of Circuit Court testimony on a hearing of May 14, 1967, file G 3284, in which Barbara Williamson was charged with operating an automobile without the owner's consent. Her sentence was probation.

"We had the F.B.I. checking on her," he said.

From Milwaukee? The Milwaukee F.B.I.?

"Well," Mike Bentzin said, "the F.B.I. has a man who comes out to all the smaller police departments. I think this man makes his rounds from Madison. What I'm telling you is what I got from the Chief."

III

It had been mentioned to me that Kromholz's sermons were fine for about six months and then that they changed. I asked Alan Kromholz if he changed his sermons. He said he did not. A woman who supported him,

---

Pat Becker, remembered that there had been a change and remembered it very specifically.

"I can remember the first one which was like a bomb. The second week in September. My mother-in-law was with me and she's not for this at all." She chuckled. "My husband took her to Madison that day."

He hadn't preached civil rights before that? I asked.

"He had never laid it on the line. Not like saying, it wasn't like saying, 'As most of you know, I've been marching in Milwaukee with Father Groppi.'"

That was the first time he'd said it?

"I don't think anybody knew he'd been," Pat Becker said. "There might have been five people who knew Al had been in marching. He said it to the whole church like. *I* didn't know it. Well, what he said, he'd been marching with Father Groppi. He kept confronting them with this. And then he said that he would let them ask questions and so forth. Well, then after that he kept giving why he was doing this with Father Groppi and so on and so forth.

"They all got excited and of course he kept it up then."

I asked what his sermons had been about before that.

"Oh, I'm sure he had civil rights in it and all this sort of thing. Steve Evans [the minister who immediately preceded Kromholz] did this too, and they were getting angry with Steve Evans. But no, nobody had ever —" Pat Becker said the following with a sing-song emphasis. "*Alan* just put it right on the *line*. Prior [to this] they could ignore it or pretend that he never said it."

This sermon became rather famous. One congregation member, Peg Buckland, said, "I understand this one service where he and McQuoid ran down the aisle, screeched or something. It sounded just horrible. They were trying to bring out some point but I was not there and I don't know enough about it. Somebody that you interview maybe could clue you in on that. Seems what they did was so disrespectful and really quite removed from anything to do with the church."

Another congregation member said, "I was at one sermon when he got off the pulpit which didn't bother me a bit. I thought it was great. It was on Milwaukee. This was around those first marches. He got off the pulpit and wanted to know if there were questions or anything. Frank van der Hoogt asked a question and I didn't really think it was too heated until I got home and my goodness, the phone was ringing and somebody was very upset about this because they thought it was completely wrong that he'd gotten out of the pulpit. But it hadn't fazed us one way or the other."

Frank van der Hoogt remembered the sermon. "I have to admit, I put my foot in my mouth once in awhile. I might point out a specific Sunday in church. I have a hard time sitting down when I think something's going on that *demands* some kind of an answer. I got up in church one time when Alan Kromholz was out of the pulpit, shaking his fist a bit at the congregation and telling them that if they didn't get with it, he meant the black situation, that we were gonna burn. And he didn't mean in hell, he meant our homes."

Are those really the kind of terms he used?

"Yes, I would say that's a fairly accurate description of words he used. In other words he said, 'You either, like get with it, or you're gonna get burned out.' This is about exactly the words he used."

Mike Bentzin was at the sermon. "He said he wouldn't use oak for protection and if you have anything to say — as much as to say, it looked like he was antagonizing to fight. I was sitting on the aisle and he kept walking up and down and looking at me, antagonizing me, and Joy kept saying, 'Don't you get up, don't you get up.' And nobody would ask any questions. He kept provoking the congregation on open housing and marching in Milwaukee, so I was ready to get up and go out. Finally Frank van der Hoogt asked him a question, he figured he better do something, it was way over the time that we usually leave. Then there were a few more questions. Oh, he was just giving everyone the devil for not marching, not getting involved and all this."

Alan Kromholz said he remembered very little about that sermon. "It was an attempt to dialogue on a Sunday with the parish about fair housing, open housing, and what was happening in Milwaukee and to raise the question whether or not it had *any* relationship to us."

Didn't you know it would be very shocking to them, to get down?

"Why should it be very shocking?"

Because ministers don't do that, I said.

Kromholz chuckled. "Okay. It really wasn't a question of is it going to be very shocking. I didn't ask that question. I don't recall asking that question. It's a method of dialogue, right? To change the physical setting. The minister always gets up into the pulpit and everyone always goes to sleep. Roughly. So, I decided that first of all we weren't going to have that climate, where they go to sleep and I try to talk about something significant. So I came off, out of the pulpit.

"And I think that sermon served its purpose. We did have dialogue. And Frank van der Hoogt got very involved in that, I think. He was saying, 'I'm there, I'm part of it,' and he was at least I think either trying to identify or maybe to confess. He was getting involved. And youth got involved. Of course the Mayor tried to leave. That's evident. He tried to get up and leave. His wife pulled him back down. I didn't do anything.

"But what about the sermon? I don't see anything."

I asked if he thought it was successful even if the dialogue invoked hatred.

"Sure. 'Cause the hatred would be there anyway. Now they started talking which is one of the things we wanted to do, have people talk."

And did you consider this an outstanding event in your ministry?

"No."

In September, at the height of Father Groppi's marches, Al Kromholz set up a series of four "Crisis-Issue" seminars for adults, sponsored by the church's Board of Christian Education. The first one was held on September 21. The speakers were Barbara Williamson, a commando secretary of Father Groppi, and Dave Rohlfing, a minister in the inner city of Milwaukee. The seminar climaxed when a congregation member, Frank van der Hoogt, was called a bigot by Barbara Williamson. Kromholz remembered her words as, "You, sir, are a bigot."

Frank van der Hoogt, in his late forties, runs a small stained glass factory in Milwaukee, has the same crew-cut he wore in the Air Force, likes William Buckley and is considered to be a bit of an intellectual. The van der Hoogts have lived in town for twenty-two years. Van remembered the time he ran into someone downtown about ten years ago and he didn't remember what the issue was, it was something to do with local politics, and the guy said, " 'Van der Hoogt, what are you sticking your nose in our business for?' " Van told me, "I was a newcomer.

"I have maybe some weird ideas sometimes, I consider myself a political conservative. I'm for smallness, whether it be in business or what not. The way mergers are going today, I just hate to see this. I like the little guy, just like I like the little guy that ran the grocery store where my kids go in and pick out the chocolate cookies. Yes, it was Mike Bentzin as a matter of fact. And Mike was a terror in this town to some people but I would say our experience with him was all good. Although he said and did things that we couldn't stand.

"Just like I go to the National Tea Store and I'm supposed to get a three-way bulb. I hate to shop and I'll always remember this. I look for a three-way bulb, certain watts, they don't have it on the shelf. I look around, there isn't anybody there, there isn't anybody to ask. I have to leave, without the three-way bulb. I wish there was a guy

I could go up to and say, look I need a three-way bulb and he'd say, 'Got some in the basement.'

"I would say I'm for smallness, that's the main thing, in government, churches, what have you," Frank van der Hoogt said.

I asked about bigness in defense spending.

"Defense spending I put in a different category because it's national security and couldn't be done locally."

Speaking of the recent invasion of Cambodia I said that it seemed that President Nixon had taken power in his own hands in violation of the conservative principle of no central control.

Van replied that you have to qualify so many things and that while he was sympathetic to Nixon, but not a nut about him, he thought there is certain information that the President has access to that the public doesn't and cannot have, and it is on this basis that he makes his decisions.

As for "bigness" in welfare payments he said, "I'll bet a lot of people on welfare if they really tried and went doorknocking could get jobs. Not all. And women with children have to be taken care of. And women deserted by alcoholic husbands and women with alcoholic husbands. But people lose pride. And I think most people today try to get more than they give.

"Now I don't want you to think I'm bragging because I'm not but I was eligible a number of years ago to receive workmen's compensation but I chose not to even though I could have because I wanted to do it on my own. Wanted to be able to say, well, not say but to know that I had never drawn it. Now most people won't do that.

"One of our daughters was born with club feet, both the soles turned in and when she was five days old she was in casts up to her hips. And she stayed in it for a long time. Then she had braces and special shoes for many years and then she finally got rid of the braces, then the shoes. Well, when she was still an infant the city nurse came and told us we were eligible for state help. But we decided not to do it, we could do it ourselves. And of course we were in debt to doctors but we finally paid them. She cost us $2,500 for her first year.

"See, maybe you could say I was brought up a little weirdly. My mother died when I was born and my father when I was nine. And then I lived with my step-mother. Well, this was in the Depression and my father had lost everything, just like those guys who jumped out of windows. And so my stepmother was left with three children, very little insurance, and this big home in Wau-watosa. All our neighbors had fathers who were still working and bringing in an income. I was out selling suet cages, bird houses, flower seeds, I peddled papers and did yard work, and homework always came last. But this property was all my stepmother had, the only bright spot in her life so she wouldn't sell it.

"Well anyway we never went to doctors, you might go to a doctor if you were dying but otherwise — never. Anyway, to this day to my knowledge I have never taken a pill of any kind. Well yes, I had shots in the army but I've never taken a pill, not even an aspirin. Maybe when I was 2½ somebody gave me one, but to my knowledge I've never taken one. In fact, this was the cause of maybe the biggest fight I ever had with my wife. This one day I had a toothache and she starts telling me how good aspirin is for a toothache and she kept nagging and nag-ging and finally I got so mad, I hardly ever yell at my wife, I slammed my fist on the kitchen table and yelled, 'Goddamn it,' I hardly ever use a cuss word. 'Goddamn it,' I yelled, 'give me the aspirin. I'll have an aspirin.'

"And she grabbed the aspirin bottle away and said, 'No, you can't have it.' And I roared, 'Give me it, I want it.' And she said, 'No, you can't have it.' And she wouldn't give me the bottle and awhile later my toothache went away.

"She saved me that time. I think they'd have to tie my arms and put me in a straitjacket before I'd ever take an aspirin now."

I asked Frank van der Hoogt what had happened at the first Crisis-Issue seminar.

"Let's put it very briefly," he said. "This inner core minister and this Barbara came to give a talk. At this meeting, maybe there were seventy-five there, most of these people are very local and most of them wouldn't drive on Twelfth and Walnut Street for all the money in the world. So they sit there and listen to this speech that these people have apparently been giving all over the state, and I'm sitting there thinking I know a little more than most of the people in the audience and getting more and more angry at what they're saying because I think it's quite wrong.

"Well, first of all they called it a disturbance, not a riot. I don't really remember too many of the details, but just basically when Barbara got up to speak she began by slurring the place where the riots started, which was around Tenth and Center Street, in Milwaukee, in one or two taverns, and added, and these are her exact words, 'owned by Jews.' So she started with this. So now she has knocked the fact that Jews own the taverns near the center. And from there she knocked the police of course, the mayor, the aldermen, the Polish people, and her whole speech to me was just strictly a big mess.

"So when she sat down, I get up with my big mouth again and said, 'It seems to me after listening to your speech that you are more prejudiced than the people you're criticizing, because in turn you have knocked the Jewish people, and all police, and city officials, and Polish people —' I don't know that I said too much more than that except that I did say that I do work very close to the core area, I work within the core area, I know people in the core area personally, black and white, and I would be willing to take a day off from my job, a full day, and take Barbara and the minister and start making calls with them and let them talk to people I know who would refute the story they were telling, so that they did not repeat the same kind of story in their next speeches. Well, this offer was never accepted. And I was serious, I wasn't putting on any kind of a show. I really meant it. I would take a day off and take them around to people I know, I'm sure they would refute most of the things these people said.

"But the end of the whole deal happened when Barbara got up and very angrily called me a bigot. And that was the end of the meeting."

Sydney McQuoid, the daughter of Weir and Vivian McQuoid, said, "I think I was the only youth there, or one of the very few. And she was a secretary to Father Groppi, and Dave Rohlfing gave a big part of the speech and then she was talking about what Father Groppi was trying to do in Milwaukee and then Mr. van der Hoogt brought up that he worked in the ghetto area, I guess he brought up that he goes in every day and he sees all of this and he feels sorry for it but it's very hard for him to have any problem or to even try to be involved in it when he lives in town and he goes back. And she was getting angry because she was saying that's the problem, all the people work in there and take the money out and bring it back to small communities or suburbs or something and she says, well, you're just *stealing* it from our people and then he went on and on, and she called him a bigot which I thought was pretty justifiable, the way he had been talking. I got terribly embarrassed for him, I remember that, when he was talking because it was just reeking out of him, it was just flowing out of him whether he wanted it to or not, it just really did."

Frank van der Hoogt said, "Now subsequent to this I had people come up to me and say, and this happened at a high school meeting I'd gone to, they came up and they pat me on the back. You know why they pat me on the back? They think I'm a bigot like they are. And these people actually detest open housing, they wouldn't live next to a black for anything. They hear these little bits of information from somebody and they say, 'Atta boy, Van, you really told them.' Well, this gets me angry too."

V

On September 28 the Watertown Chief of Police, Marlyn Mann, also a member of the congregation, spoke at the second Crisis-Issue seminar in the church. He is a nice-looking man in his middle forties with dark wetly combed hair. On the wall of his office are two sets of pictures of former Watertown police chiefs and a large mounted fish. On the ledge next to the window is a three foot high copper and wood bullet.

I first met the police chief at Mayor Bentzin's suggestion. Bentzin said, "I want you to meet the police chief and I want the Chief to meet you." Bentzin drove me over and introduced us.

The Chief told me, "We have plenty of files on Mr. Kromholz but I warn you, you may find this shocking."

When I later went back to speak to the Chief he told me they had recently destroyed the files since there was no reason to keep them. Although he could give me little information about what was in the files, "just some license plate numbers," Chief Mann was congenial and talkative. He told me several stories about the nature of police work.

Mann said that people are going berserk everyday, citing the case of a man in Watertown who took a hatchet to his friend and split his head open but didn't kill him. The man then ran upstairs and the police had him completely covered with their high-power rifles but didn't fire a shot because at that point no innocent life was in danger. A lieutenant walked up the stairs to get the man and the man fired right at the lieutenant and missed him by an inch. "Strangely enough he said he'd talk with me," Mann said, and so he went up the stairs. Mann insisted that the man put his gun down and he did but remained crouched over it. "As soon as I got to the top I kicked the gun away and had him handcuffed. The upshot was that he got six months and was let off free. It makes you wonder," Chief Mann said. "We spend so many hours and so much time bringing these people in and then the courts let them go. But we can't be judge and jury too. We're caught in the middle. And I mean the middle. There's a lot of cases of berserkness and light sentences. They get freed right after."

Mann then told of a fifteen-year-old girl who was murdered by a seventeen- and a nineteen-year-old. "She got two bullets in the back of her head and one in the eye as she was lying there." One of the boys got a light sentence and the other one was let off free.

He also told me of a boy who was mad at his parents and shot his mother and father and buried his mother under hay in the barn and his father under a manure pile. "He got six months, not even in jail, and then he was let free," Mann said.

The Chief then told me how closely they have to stick to the law. They used to be able to pick up vagrants and give them a meal and a place to stay at night. They called them "lodgers." Mann said, "Naturally we had to lock the cell because you can't tell if the guy was planted or something. You can't just have a stranger walking around the cells at night. Well, one time a lodger had a heart attack in his cell and when they found him he was dead. His family started a lawsuit and collected $400,000." That set a precedent and it is impossible to have lodgers now. "There are [police] inspectors who come out and immediately say, 'Show me the cells.' First thing," Mann said. "And if there's any man locked up who doesn't have his arrest papers, the jail can be shut down or given a huge fine. And the inspectors always love to come in the middle of the night. So lodgers are a thing of the past."

We spoke about general principles of law enforcement. "The F.B.I. says if your gun is justified, when you shoot, shoot to kill. Do you know how most policemen are lost each year? They wound a man and he's lying there and they go up to him and he has his hand on his gun and blows their head off."

I asked if it wasn't possible to just shoot in some part of the body that would disable but not kill.

"Where?" Mann asked. "In the arm, he can still run and shoot. In the leg, he can too. The only place that would disable is the spine. You *have* to shoot to kill.

"Now they say brutal types go into law enforcement. But a police officer has to be neutral. There was this march in Milwaukee and the police were escorting the marchers and they came back full of spit. This isn't something I heard; I saw it with my own eyes. There was this colored woman, weighed about three hundred pounds. Well, she came up to this officer. Hadn't blown her nose in about six months and she comes up and picks her nose and put a big glob right on his shirt and he doesn't move. He wasn't supposed to. There were four TV cameras right on him. They *knew* it was gonna happen, just trying to create an incident.

"Well, I woulda hit her. I know you're not supposed to but I would take that from no one. Anyway, this guy didn't bat an eyelash."

Mann told me there is no discrimination in Watertown. "Now I wouldn't say there's any discrimination. Once we had a Mexican come in and ask for an application for the police examination — we give it twice a year, and of course I gave it to him. And of course he flunked the test miserably. Then he took it again and barely passed. And when his name came up before the board I said, 'Oh, strike him.' *Not* because he was Mexican but because of his accent. He was really hard to understand. I knew he'd be heckled by the town kids and what if there was a fight and he had to break it up? I knew he'd break into Spanish if he was excited and we couldn't have that could we? Now if there were more Mexicans in town I wouldn't hesitate for a minute but as it was — "

Chief Mann told me about the time he spoke at the church's Second Crisis-Issue seminar.

"Kromholz called me once and asked me to speak on the relationship of law enforcement and the church and I said sure, I'd be delighted to, and then awhile later I received in the mail a thing announcing a four-speaker series ten-dollar-a-plate dinner and Father Groppi was the first speaker. And that was the first I heard about that. I was tricked into it," Chief Mann said.

"Anyway, usually there's a twenty-minute question and answer period after the speech and I spoke for two hours and forty minutes — questions and answers, that is — and the audience was hostile, very hostile. They weren't too much in favor of law enforcement. And one of the big questions that arose was as to why I had purchased certain things for riot equipment such as your riot helmets, your riot sticks, high-powered rifles, shotguns, so on and so forth and tear gas, and what right did I have to purchase this equipment with the taxpayers' money when some of these taxpayers could be demonstrators and this equipment would be used against them? And that we had no right under any conditions in case of a demonstration to take this equipment and *use* it against the demonstrators. Now naturally we are not gonna come out there with shotguns and high powered rifles against these demonstrators. It may be necessary to use tear gas."

I asked why they had purchased the high-powered rifles.

Mann said, "Our weapons were in a very depleted condition here in the department. They were old, they weren't up to date. And what I had in mind at the time I purchased this equipment was we were having quite a few of these cases where the individuals would get up into a tower or into a building and they would start sniping. Now what I have in mind here is this case that took place down in Texas where this mentally deranged person got up in this tower of the university and I forget whether he killed —"

I interrupted, Wasn't this about the time of a lot of riots too?

"Right," Mann said. "And I think he shot and killed eleven people, I might be wrong, and he wounded, I think there were thirty-six people involved. Eleven were killed and the rest wounded. And this is what I had in mind.

"Now look, here's what I say. I'm not saying I know how to preach. I'm not saying I know how to do brain surgery, or take out an appendix. But I do know about law enforcement. And I don't tell a minister how to preach. But that's the trouble — seems like everyone's trying to tell the police how to do law enforcement. In law enforcement you have to be neutral. An alderman gets a ticket around here, he pays it, or he goes to court. Police officers are here to protect life and property. I don't care who's making a fuss. And I told them, if there's rioters and they're looting, they should be shot. Warn them but if they don't stop, they should be shot. They don't loot for the reasons they say. They loot to loot."

In the written text of the speech Mann had given at the seminar was the sentence, "We cannot and will not fail to enforce any law on the books because we think it unwise or unjust." I read the sentence to him and asked, "What would happen if there was a law you didn't agree with, that you deeply disagreed with?"

Mann replied, "We are charged with the protection of life and property. We have the duty to arrest anyone breaking the law. It is not our duty to rehabilitate. It's not our job or within our capabilities. But if a man breaks a law, I don't care who he is, if he's black, white, yellow, checkered, rich, poor, if he breaks the law he has to be arrested. And if we don't enforce the law then we are negligent. We *have* to enforce it. There is no choice."

At the seminar the question of police brutality was raised. Dave Fries, city attorney at the time and not a member of the congregation, remembered. "I think I heckled him a little, for one thing," Fries said. "He gave a rather non-ideological presentation, but he was glorifying and justifying the purchase and use of mace and riot equipment, helmets, shotguns and all the rest of this, but it was put on the basis that they needed more men to put on the police force. For example he felt that he needed more than three men on the midnight-to-eight shift, and I agreed with that. He felt that we needed at least two patrol cars plus a man at the desk, and so he built from that base and gave the impression, I think, that this is a bastion against invading black hordes, without openly stating it. I'm not sure if this is the idea that gets through to people or if I'm just a paranoid about it. Undoubtedly a bit of both. And I was critical of him in some degree — I'd just been reading *The Big Blue Line,* a book about police brutality around the country, so I was full of that stuff. Also full of indignation because a friend that I visited in the hospital in Milwaukee said that she had been marching with Groppi and was at one of Groppi's church services one night during the time when the police were being very — oppressive. She was walking to her car, a block or two away from there, and a police car came up and a man rolled down the window and said, 'Have you been to church?' and she said yes and he said, 'Get in, you're under arrest.' I thought it was pretty blatant to put it that way! And I think I cited that to the group assembled as an indication that the police are not always right. I indicated for example that the police officers in Milwaukee remove their badges so that when they do all these things they can't be picked on. I think that's just about when that technique was starting. Of course, it's an old thing now."

Chief Mann said, "Somebody brought up the fact of police brutality. So I asked this group, I said is there anybody here who has ever been mistreated by a policeman or anybody in law enforcement? And of course there was no one. And I said is there anybody here who has actually witnessed any police brutality, a police officer beating someone unmercifully for no reason. I said naturally we do have hostile prisoners and we do have to use force to bring this man under control, by this I don't mean beating him over the head and pounding him into the ground.

"So this one individual we're talking about here [Kromholz] mentioned that he was a victim of police brutality. And I asked him in what manner he was a victim of police brutality. Now this is how things get so miscon-strued. He claimed that he was down in either Mississippi or Georgia on a march down there, for the rights of these colored people to vote. He said he was beat up on the streets of this community at 10:30 in the morning, in broad daylight. And he had some teeth knocked out, and I don't know what all happened. Now, mind you he was beat up at 10:30 in the morning. And I said, 'Well, what hap-pened?'

"'Well,' he said, 'I was just minding my own busi-ness,' and he says, 'I was beat up, knocked down, kicked, and everything.'

"I said, 'By police officers, police officers did this to you? You were walking down the street minding your own business, you weren't in the march or anything, just walking down the street and you were beat up by police officers?'

"'Well, no,' he says, 'I wasn't beat up by police officers, I was beat up by some of the citizens down there.'

"And I said, 'Well how do you get police brutality out of this?'

"'Well,' he said, 'there was a squad car about a block, block and a half down the street and they never looked back.'

"They were going in the opposite direction by the way — they never looked back, they never came to his aid. Well, I know I can't see that much in my rear-view mirror and I can't see a fight a block and a half in back. So this is police brutality. I mean he said this in front of this whole group."

Open Housing I

The Crisis-Issue Seminars were set against a backdrop
of great social movement in the state. Not only in Milwaukee, but throughout Wisconsin there was a movement to adopt local fair housing ordinances. Although
there was a state open housing law, it covered only
twenty-five percent of the existing housing units in the
state and exempted all single dwelling units occupied by
the owner (or vacant units which were last occupied by
the owner), and all rooming and apartment houses with
four or less units in which the owner resided.

In the middle of September Watertown's city attorney, Dave Fries, received a letter from the administra-
tor of the Equal Rights Division of the state's Department
of Industry, Labor and Human Relations with a model
fair housing ordinance enclosed and a recommendation
that it be adopted. The model ordinance was drafted by
the state attorney general, Bronson La Follette.

Early in October the Frieses, with their friends
and neighbors the Kromholzes, attended a meeting of a
liberal Catholic group at St. Henry's Catholic Church. At

this meeting Fries stated that he was going to recommend an open housing ordinance to the City Council. He did this several weeks later.

On October 8 Al Kromholz, one of the driving powers behind the effort to pass local housing legislation in Watertown, asked the president of the League of Women Voters if the League would support open housing. After checking with their state board and getting an enthusiastic response, they did. The League then ran a series of three articles on open housing starting on October 21 in the *Watertown Daily Times*.

This was the first point of real involvement for two of Kromholz's strongest supporters in the congregation, Frank and Kathy Isaacson. Mrs. Isaacson, who was the president of the League, told me the involvement came about almost by accident. In the fall the Kromholzes stayed for dinner and "the conversation just kind of pulled us in to Al's side." It was then he told them he was marching with Father Groppi. The Isaacsons had not been attending church but then found themselves working with Kromholz to support fair housing. Later in the year Frank Isaacson was on a number of important church committees.

"We didn't charge in expecting to give everybody light and reason and show them our side was the best," said Kathy Isaacson, a tall striking woman in her twenties. "We were sort of just pulled into it. It wasn't the man, it was the issue. And confrontation politics haven't been entirely disproven. It seemed reasonable enough."

On October 11 the Watertown Methodist Church's Official Board recommended to the City Council the drawing up of a local housing law. This was passed unanimously by the thirty-five members present.

On October 13 Dave Fries wrote to Mayor Bentzin a letter (which was also sent to the councilmen) in which he recommended the adoption of La Follette's model fair housing ordinance.

The Watertown City Council meets two nights a week. Monday night is their committee meeting when they decide what action they will take in their public meeting on Tuesday night. On Monday night, October 16, the Council decided to refer the issue of open housing to the Council's committee on public welfare. That committee was headed by Alderman Charles Yeomans, a member of the Congregational Church. According to the October 17 *Daily Times*, Yeomans said that the committee would begin its study immediately and would probably file a report with the Council in about a month. He said that copies of similar ordinances adopted in Madison and Beloit would also be obtained and studied. The article concluded:

Mayor Bentzin expressed the opinion that the move by La Follette was "a political gimmick" but this was disputed by the city attorney.

Several aldermen added their thoughts to the discussion and what eventually emerged is that it is certain the council is going to go slowly in the matter and that a study by the committee, which is to be authorized at tonight's session, is the first step in that direction.

Individual aldermen, along with the city attorney, agreed that they had heard of no cases of discrimination in housing on the local level.

I asked Mayor Bentzin about the issue. He said, "We don't have problems here. We don't have coloreds. At the time it was very popular to pass open housing even though there's a federal law and there's no need to pass it if you don't have a problem, is there? We don't have any problem here. There's only one colored family here and they're both old. There's always been a colored family here. They worked down at the barbershop. The one with six chairs. Shoeshine. There's no discrimination here, there was always the colored man who shined shoes and when he didn't work he brought in his friend and so on until Mr. Goodie decided to live here, and he raised his kids here. 'Course they're [the kids] gone now, but when

Mrs. Goodie was sick do you know Mr. Goodie wrote a letter to the paper thanking people for how kind they had been. [And] we have lots of Mexican-Americans from Clyman who work at the canning factory living here. They like it here. And no one's ever been actually turned down for a house and it's covered by state and federal law so why do we need it here? Just because everyone's doing it — You wouldn't have a traffic light in the middle of the desert would you?"

On October 17, the day of the City Council meeting, thirteen ministers issued a statement endorsing open housing and also took out a paid advertisement in the *Daily Times* with the same statement. The thirteen were a majority of the association of Watertown ministers, the Clergy Round Table, which had been unable to come to an agreement to endorse open housing as an organization. The statement read:

AS MEMBERS OF THE CHURCH OF JESUS CHRIST, WE AFFIRM
> The Fatherhood of God and the brotherhood of man;
> The love of God and the justice of his Gospel in Jesus Christ;
> Our personal responsibility to all our fellow men.

WE RECOGNIZE
1. The leadership and initiative of Madison and Beloit who have recently enacted fair housing ordinances.
2. Our responsibility to declare openly and forthrightly the conviction of the rightness of municipal fair housing ordinances for our community and other communities in our state.

WE COMMIT OURSELVES
1. To work with all our resources and abilities for a fair housing ordinance for Watertown;
2. To declare in word and deed complete dignity and self respect for all human beings as creatures of God.

The first of the thirteen signatures was Alan Krom-holz's. I asked him why Watertown needed a fair housing ordinance and Kromholz told me that first of all the state law was not all-inclusive and local ordinances were necessary not only for the community itself but in order to put pressure on the state legislature to pass a state law. "Secondly," he said, "I saw, or I believe that the small communities of our state are simply feeders of racial prejudice and conservative attitudes and bigotry — into the cities. All the young boys and girls leave the small town and where do they go? They go to the large metropolitan centers of the country. Milwaukee, for example. The attitudes that they grew up hearing and believing and now espousing were the attitudes of racism. It had to be confronted there in the local community. If the community is not equipped to stand and say we believe in integration, and in open housing, in freedom, in peace and not war, what effect would it ever have on their children or on the metropolitan areas that are having problems?"

There were other endorsements. Father Vincent Thilman of St. Bernard's Catholic Church said, "When the whole question come up here in town about whether there should be an open housing ordinance for our city, well, Al and I were both quite active in trying to get it through the Council, you see, hmm? Even our own Rosary Altar Society, which usually doesn't do very much on social questions, voted in a meeting in favor of it, you see, which just about blew me down, but I was pleased beyond repair.

"Now the parish board dodged the issue by deciding at their meeting to bring it up at the general meeting, see. Then at the annual general meeting, everybody's invited, and it passed that meeting although that meeting created some division the following week. Because it was even brought up at that meeting. But the majority that were there were in favor of the open housing ordinance.

I don't say there wasn't a little planning on that." He laughed. "That's the way the vote went. 'Course they were put on the spot the way the vote was, might have been different if it was a secret ballot. It's hard to say. But people don't like to put their hands up and say, 'I'm prejudiced.' But there were a lot of people in the parish that were really fighting for it, see."

Al Kromholz did not have such luck in his own church. On November 7 a resolution supporting open housing was introduced to the Church Council, which is the executive council of the church and has representatives from the other church boards. Although one board, the Diaconate, went on record as supporting the open housing resolution, two boards had not discussed the matter and instructed their representatives, and a motion was made to hold the resolution in abeyance until the following month.

II

It is not unimportant to know that the city attorney, Dave Fries, a friend of Alan Kromholz, and the man who first recommended to the City Council that they pass open housing, is chairman of the Socialist Party of Wisconsin. He is commonly regarded as a Communist.

One congregation member told me, "He [Kromholz] was extremely close to this Fries who they say is a very active Communist."

Michael Bausch, a college student and member of the congregation said that the men in City Hall "are convinced that the former city attorney, Fries, they're convinced that he's a card-carrying Communist. He may be, I don't know. But all this stuff was floating around and all this was tied in with Kromholz. They may have had associations somewhere along the line — guilt by association."

Mike Bentzin said, "I got this from the Police Chief: he [Kromholz] was hanging around with the only fellow in Watertown that if there was a foreign invasion, he'd be picked up immediately. The F.B.I. told him [Mann] that."

Betty Ebert, a congregation member, told me that Joy Bentzin had said to her, " 'And he [Kromholz] goes around with David Fries, and you know that he's an *admitted* Communist.' Oh, she'd said 'an atheistic card-carrying Communist.' And I said, 'Hey, you're using some pretty strong language there. What do you mean?' 'Well,' she said, 'for one thing at the City Council meetings he does *not* enter into the invocation, he will not be a part of it. That makes him an atheist.' And I said 'that makes him an atheist because he doesn't want to participate in the invocation?' and she said 'Well, everybody else bows their heads and he doesn't even come until it's over.' And then I said, 'And what makes him a Communist?' and she said, 'He does *not* repeat the Pledge of Allegiance to the flag.' Well, my own son won't do that. And I said, 'Oh, that makes him a Communist?' and she said, 'Well you know he's one, you know it's right in the paper, he calls himself one.' "

I asked Dave Fries about the invocation at Council meetings.

He said, "I dislike public prayer, with a hypocritical nature particularly, because they have the prayer at the Tuesday night meeting but not at the Monday night meeting. The Monday night meeting is when they decide what they're going to do at the Tuesday night meeting, so that's the significant meeting when the invocation of divine guidance should be sought, if they actually feel that they are getting some divine guidance through this ritual. And I feel it can be opposed on two grounds, the humanist atheist view that I adopt, or the true religious believer who would regard it as hypocrisy."

I asked on what grounds he opposed it as a humanist atheist.

"Well," Dave Fries said, "I just don't believe in the efficacy of prayer and I think it tends to demean public life to have a bunch of phonies who reject all the teachings of the world's great religions pretend that they adhere to them."

And the Pledge of Allegiance?

"I'm not interested in pledging to the flag particularly. Because the flag right now of course is a symbol in my eyes of the disgrace that America has suffered in Vietnam. It has been used as a justification for too many crimes. It'll take a long time before this will ever be restored even to the rank that polite people ought to pay *any* attention to it, in my eyes. And of course also from the internationalist standpoint, I don't like nationalism, I don't like the idea that you teach people to respect the flag and then expect them to go out docilely, and expect them to get killed, for the women to wave the handkerchiefs tearfully as they go off. So I was accustomed most Council meetings of timing my arrival about 7:35. Much of this was not merely by design. We were busy with our younger son on a program of therapy we had for him and it took time and I found that by the time I got to the meeting it was about that time. I'd usually be coming up the stairs and I heard all this stuff, and I'd wait until it was concluded, and I'd go in as everyone was shuffling chairs and coughing, and I'd sit down. And Bentzin, I suppose, thought this was disgraceful."

Do you consider yourself a Communist? I asked.

Fries laughed. "Oh, not a Communist. A Socialist. It's not an economic difference. I suppose economically I could be a Communist but politically I regard Communists as essentially not believers in democracy. 'Course in Czechoslovakia there was the beginnings of an effort toward a democratic Communism. It might have been a very interesting process if it had been allowed to occur."

Fries told me he had been a member of the Young Republicans until 1950 when he broke with the party over

Joe McCarthy. Then he worked in the Democratic Party and in the A.D.A. "Until the war came, and then I had to do something, as an individual, even if I was the only one that knew. So I joined the Socialist Party then." He told me that since then he has found a substantial element in the Socialist Party that is willing to overlook the war in order to maintain friendship with the labor movement and in that respect they're not much better than many Democrats.

III

On October 18, the following letter from Watertown attorney Bernard Traeger appeared in the *Watertown Daily Times:*

> The proposal that Watertown adopt a "fair housing" ordinance is, in effect, a proposal to endorse the riots, vandalism, prevarication and desecration by Milwaukee's Public Enemy Number One and his private army. If we endorse them, we, in effect, suggest to others that they join this mob of juvenile delinquents, convicted criminals, and social misfits for additional blackmail by Black Power.

Traeger's second paragraph said it was already illegal in Wisconsin to discriminate "by refusing to sell, lease, etc. because of race, etc," and that in two years of the law's existence only thirty-five complaints of violation were made, "seven of which were thrown out as baseless. Of the remaining twenty-eight cases, there has been one conviction, and some cases are pending." He continued:

> We do not become alarmed when Poles, Germans, etc., live in nationality groups in our large cities, or when Norwegians or Swiss dominate the population of some of our smaller cities. It seems to be the nature of man to want to live in homogeneous groups in a heterogeneous country. Though we recognize advantages and disadvantages, we neither forbid nor require people to live in such groups. It would appear from the fact that only 28 bona fide complaints have been made in

two years that most, or all, of these people who wanted to leave the concentrated areas have been able to do so. The fact that the Negro, for the most part, does not choose to leave is an indication, to some extent, of race pride. We should encourage such pride, and not discourage it. In towering numbers, Negroes are climbing to the top of all fields of endeavor, and the success of each additional one develops more racial pride.

It is not proper, therefore, to suggest that the Negro is such bad company for himself that he should not be permitted to live among his own, if he prefers to do so. It is also improper to prevent him from leaving the concentrated area, if he chooses; and to that end, there has been protective legislation. If we are truly interested in helping the Negro, rather than to give power to the Guerrillas, we should concentrate on improving conditions within the area where he wants to live.

Traeger then said that the open housing law treads upon the dangerous ground of policing of men's minds "to see whether he has turned a Negro away because of prejudice or for some other reason." He said that the gentlemen of the far left raised loud objections to loyalty oaths, which, Traeger said, was mind reading in matters of loyalty to the United States. But now the same groups seem to be advocating thought control — an amazing reversal on the part of the leftists. He concluded:

There is absolutely no way one can prevent a Negro from buying a piece of real estate anywhere in Wisconsin. As a last resort, he could have his white friend buy it for him, and resell it to him. There are greater problems with renting, because some of the elements, that are now tearing Milwaukee apart to get open housing, are people who could justly be refused housing by landlords, not because of their color but because of their bad records.

Groppi's Puppies, who so playfully chewed up Milwaukee's City Hall, will probably start snarling at ours. Usually, an ordinance is enacted to fulfill a demonstrated need. We have had no incident suggesting a need. We have a state law that is applicable here in Watertown. Our only purposes in passing the law would be to endorse guerrilla warfare, or possibly to let a man be tried twice for the same offense.

Let's get on with more needed and pressing legislation — such as a safety ordinance requiring annual wheel alignment in motor-powered unicycles!

Father Vincent Thilman had mentioned this letter to me. He said, "Well, during this period of time the town was just torn apart and so, a lot of things happened. One of the lawyers in town, who should have known better, put in the paper a letter to the editor that there was already a state law on this matter and there's no necessity of us having a city law on the matter. Yes, Traeger. And so we were working with our eighth grade civics club, with Sister Judith at the time, and so in the discussion they had come around to, well, why don't we write a letter, since we had told them that the state law only covered twenty-five percent of housing. And so they wrote a letter in answer to Mr. Traeger's letter saying that even we eighth graders know that the law only covers twenty-five percent. And of course some people in the parish thought we were corrupting *our* youth see? Because of *truth* you see hmm?"

I spoke with Bernard Traeger in his law office. He is in his early fifties, has a full round face, and is extremely cordial. He gave me a copy of the above letter and another he wrote in December 1967. "You can read this over more at your leisure," he said, "but this particular article is a summary of my whole opinion on the thing. It was the same then as it is now. It'll never change because these are basic truths as far as I'm concerned. To my way of thinking Father Groppi is a very serious criminal who is teaching crime to a lot of unhappy and neglected people, and people who are willing to accept a false doctrine. And he has got a lot of people in trouble. We had four people killed in our riots which had happened this very summer [1967]."

How was he connected with the riot? I asked.

"How was he connected with the riots? 'Course you weren't here. Father Groppi led this group for two hundred successive days on a march. They'd go here and they'd go there. They'd go down and molest the Polacks on the south side of Milwaukee. And the Polacks would then march up and molest the Negroes in the so-called core area. I avoid the word ghetto. To me ghetto is a term that applies to a Jewish area in a European country where the Jews were forced by law to live in an area. And I think ghetto is an inappropriate term. The ghetto was a very cruel thing to the Jews and I don't believe that we have this ghetto for the Negro. I believe that the Negro is imprisoned by what he hears from the mouth of Groppi. These people are free to come out here to Watertown. We had it happen.

"There's a Mr. Goodie in town, a very fine gentleman, a family of artists. He and his wife were active in the Methodist Church, they came out here to perform, they were treated with such kindness they decided to move to Watertown. He came here with his children, they all went to our high school, he must have had four of them young enough to go to our high school, and maybe four were old enough that they were through high school when the family moved here. One was an excellent drum major in our band. You know there's nobody can strut like a Negro girl. They just have it all over the whites. They're all, I shouldn't say all, I should never categorize like that, but these people are talented and they have a rhythm and so on and they were excellent musicians in the high school band. I don't think there were any athletes, I think most of them were girls. But in any event, this man commented publicly many times how well he was treated in Watertown. So we had a city where one person to my knowledge sought to come here and he was accepted and he became a Fuller Brush salesman. He's been in my home, he's been in this office. We're very fond of Mr. Goodie.

"For someone to assert that we *needed* a fair housing ordinance here, as I say here, 'ordinarily we pass an ordinance when there is some showing when we need it.'

Now what reason did we have to pass the ordinance? To satisfy Groppi, see. Now I call it a Black Mafia in one of these articles [the second article]. I was in the F.B.I. for eight years as a special agent and I worked on Mafia cases and part of the Mafia working is to give the impression if you don't cooperate you're going to get it. You better do what you're told and then look what happened to so and so. So the idea is they'd go around to these various cities, put the pressure on, and they'd get the ordinance passed and then they'd say, 'See stick with us, we get these laws passed.' Laws which didn't mean a damn thing see. Because it was already state law in Wisconsin."

Didn't it only cover twenty-five percent of housing?

"All right," Traeger said, "let's take a look at that. How many Negroes want to live in Watertown? One? Hundred? All right, twenty-five percent of our property's available. Let's assume that that's true. They going to buy a hundred percent of it? Is there any reason why a Negro cannot buy or rent housing in Watertown? Is there any evidence that he can't? What *if* only twenty-five percent is available? Frankly, a hundred percent is never available. I can't come in here and buy a hundred percent of the property, see. Now, this is one of the things. You're giving power to Groppi," he laughed, "the evil one.

"All right, I am a Catholic and this is another one of the reasons I am opposed to Groppi, he wore the Roman collar which we now call the riot collar. To me, I have a brother who is a priest, I had an uncle who was a priest, I have a niece who is a nun, to me the Catholic Church is very important, and for a *bum* like that to put on that collar and say to people, look at this beautiful house and the beautiful lawn, this should be yours — see, this is on TV. And of course his foul language I won't go into, I wouldn't repeat it. But then he would say, 'This you should have.' Thou Shalt Not Covet, you see. Then he talks about the Bible, he carried a Bible, understand. My opposition is Groppi and company, I have no objection to Negroes."

Referring to a welfare march that Groppi led Bernard Traeger said, "Down there at the welfare riot we had at Madison where he tried to, well, he put the legislature out of — well, they had to adjourn. He carried a Bible all during this time and he refers to the time Christ was in jail. Well, you can read that Bible from beginning to end and Christ was never in jail. He was in custody, in a sense, he was scourged at the pillar, so he was in custody. And he was crucified so he was in custody there but I don't believe he was in custody of any lawful authority. I mean, the Roman soldiers represented law and order and the Romans scourged him, but the Jews crucified him — or I like to get away from that too, because from a religious standpoint we all crucified him, see. But anyway I think we should down tone this that the Jews crucified Christ, but I mean it was people who happened to be Jewish, as Christ happened to be Jewish.

"Anyway, that was one point that bothered me. The only thing we would accomplish would be to build up the power of the Mafia. We have no problem here, see. If we had no automobiles in town we would need no speed limit for automobiles, right?"

Right, I said.

Traeger continued, "There were a lot of articles written that did attack me, there were a lot of people who were in my favor, and I had to laugh at some of the things they said. They didn't understand what it was all about but they were for me. Like I ended up this article, 'Let's get on with the more needed pressing legislation such as a safety ordinance requiring annual wheel alignment on motor-powered unicycles.'" He laughed. "Wheel alignment on a unicycle see. That's more important than a housing ordinance. All right, that was supposed to be a touch of humor. But one of the fellows who agreed with me said, 'Yes, let's pass this ordinance, we need it.'" Still laughing, Traeger said, "And he wasn't trying to be funny.

"So the people who are your friends — reminds me

of the old saying, 'Lord protect me from my friends, I can take care of my enemies myself.' You know you get strange bedfellows who agree with you. You're not proud of them, you see. There are some people who have bigotry in their background, but there's very little of it here in Watertown. Every once in awhile if you read it carefully you might think this person is bigoted.

"But, this is something, this is why I say the liberals aren't liberal. These people call you a bigot when you disagree with them, see. And they are not tolerant, they are not tolerant. The housing ordinance was a *bad* ordinance, in and of itself. It has nothing to do with color. But it gets in the field of mindreading.

"I don't know if it was the first or second article where I talk about mindreading. Oh yeah, you know I was in the F.B.I. from 1940 on and it was sometime after that they came along with something they called the loyalty affidavits. They were the most absurd thing that this country ever did. People and teachers in the universities were asked to sign an affidavit that they were not a member of the Communist Party, and they were not sympathetic and so on. Thought control.

"Along about that time, '45, '46 or so, Senator McCarthy, Joe McCarthy, came along. I was a Republican and I was a delegate to the state convention and I was a last-minute substitute on the resolutions committee at the state convention one year. And somebody introduced a resolution endorsing Senator McCarthy. And I opposed it all alone. There were about twenty people in a room. The press was locked out and we washed our laundry in private. Now, a lot of people would put me in the category with McCarthy and I have to laugh at it because of all the work I did to lick this sort of thing. McCarthy called everybody Communist. I said he is the worst enemy the cause of anti-Communism has. Because if you call everybody a Communist, nobody's going to believe anybody anymore when you got one, see.

"We dragged out a whole day and when I came out into — it was in the Arena in Milwaukee, my classmate from law school, Glenn Davis, was our congressman from this district then, now he's in the Waukesha district. He came over and sat down next to me and I said, 'Glenn, don't stay here too long today, I'm a very unpopular person. It isn't going to do you any good to be seen with me.'" Laughing, Traeger said, "I was ostracized from that Republican Party that day, I'm telling you. But fortunately, we did make our point, we toned it down. And I didn't want an open debate on the floor because you wash your laundry in public, you just hurt the party. But I never went to a Republican convention since, and I don't belong to the party as such. I'm a Republican in principle, but I've never gone back."

Traeger then spoke of other past experiences. He told me he lived in the South for two years from 1940 to 1942, investigating civil rights violations for the F.B.I. "The most amazing thing was I didn't find things in the South I was told I would find," he said. "I found happy Negroes, and especially so among the country Negroes. See, the city Negroes have more unhappiness because they have the Negro honky-tonk where they drink a lot of rot-gut liquor.

"I was given the impression that the Southerner's happiness was kicking the Negro around. I was amazed when I got down there to find how many people devoted a lot of time to helping Negroes. People did this in Atlanta all the time while I was there. It amazed me, it seemed inconsistent with what I'd been told in school up here.

"One of the most enlightening discussions came after I had arrested my first Negro. He was a man with a beautiful build, Joe Louis type, he was all man, you know. And they have an expression in the South that you might think is a prejudiced statement. They say he's a big buck nigger. First of all, the Southerner says nigra. Like my name's Traeger, they say Trigga. It's the way they pronounce it. Nigra is what they're saying but many of the Negroes say nigger. But if you listen closely to the Georgian, he's saying nigra. Now sometimes they mimic the Negro and say nigger. But when they say nigra, nothing intended to be insulting to anyone, see. But anyway, they called him a big buck nigra and I was a little bit shocked when I heard that term and then Mr. Meyerhart who was the United States Commissioner said to me, he said, 'Traeger, you don't understand what this is all about.' He said, 'Back in the days of slavery the plantation owner was much like your farmer in Wisconsin. Your farmer will send to New Jersey to get a bull to breed his cows with,' this was before artificial insemination. 'Well,' he says, 'so it was with the plantation owner. He wanted to breed the best type of Negro that he could.' These people were chattels, they were not people. 'So he would pick out the biggest buck Negro on his plantation and use him for breeding purposes. When it was time for a Negro woman to be bred, the buck Negro would breed her.' Then she was free to 'live up with,' and they still use this expression today, they 'live up with,' any man they chose. But after she had her child she was segregated again until she was bred again. Then she could live up with anyone.

"You see," Bernard Traeger said, "we taught the Negroes not to be married. I don't know what their custom was in Africa but I know if they had any family life, we sure as heck knocked the hell out of it in America, didn't we? And *not* because somebody wanted to be vicious but because somebody wanted to do what was economically sound to do, or let's say, agriculturally sound. See, we wanted to improve the breed, so to speak, to get a bigger and stronger Negro. And we have a lot of strong ones this day and we have a lot of runts which is because of some of the inbreeding I suppose. But we have a lot of that in other people too."

After open housing had been publicly endorsed by thirteen clergymen in the *Daily Times,* a meeting was held in
the Mayor's office between Alan Kromholz and Mike
Bentzin. Also present were Glen Siferd, a Methodist minister who had lived in Watertown only a few months, and
the Chief of Police, Marlyn Mann.

Glen Siferd said, "Al and I just decided that someone of the Clergy Round Table should go to the Mayor
and share our views on this thing, sit down and discuss it.
And so Al made the appointment for half an hour. And I
suppose I was in the meeting when they were discussing
this and I said, 'Sure, I'll go with you.' I think Al and I
were both very quiet and calm and we thought this was
just going to be a sharing of views. I had never of course
met the Mayor beforehand and I didn't really know what
to expect. As we came in Al of course took the lead because he knew the Mayor, he'd made the appointment
and so forth. He came in and the secretary announced us
and he said, 'Come in,' and then he just sat there at his
desk and did some work while we just kind of stood there.
We didn't really know what to do, and finally he said,
'I'm waiting for the Police Chief. I want him to hear
everything that goes on here because I don't trust a thing
this man says,' and he looks at Al. His pastor. How could
Bentzin have such fear of a man of God who had come to
talk about open housing? And finally the Police Chief did
come in and he sat him down and he sat us down."

You mean you were standing this whole time? I
asked.

"Yeah," Glen Siferd said. "And he left all the doors
open. One was to the secretary's office and one was to the
city offices on the other side. And I don't know, things
flared pretty quick. It was obvious that the Mayor was
emotionally involved here as we would be discussing this
thing very objectively. And he made it plain that I, having been here only a couple of months, or three, really

didn't have any business saying anything. I wouldn't know the needs of Watertown or the circumstances or anything like that. And most of the hour was just a harangue by him. I wish I had a tape recording of Bentzin at that meeting. We could have brought him to court and sued him for what he said."

Do you remember the kinds of things he said?

"Well, he indicated one time that Al Kromholz was under investigation and he would prove he was a Communist."

He said that? I asked.

"Yes."

What kind of investigation?

"He didn't indicate that," Siferd said. "But there was the Police Chief so I assume that there was collusion, or he had in mind to work through that branch. And of course he indicated violent disagreement with positions Al had taken, with his being on the march one time with Father Groppi. I'm not sure, I suppose he said something like the church should stick to the gospel and not be concerned with these other things like open housing. And I, I didn't swallow anything he said. I came back at him, but Al would sit there absolutely quietly, take any kind of abuse or misstatements."

I asked what the Chief of Police did during this.

"He was very quiet. I got the impression he was under the Mayor's thumb. Little boy who was going to do whatever he was told to. It seemed to me he was a little apologetic about the circumstance and yet he wasn't big enough or strong enough to say, as I think he should have, 'This is none of my business. If these men made an appointment with you, you're to see to it. If they want to talk to me, they can — and I'm not there to just be your puppy dog.'"

Was Siferd shocked by the whole thing?

"I'm far beyond being shocked by anything like this. I was angered and I was ashamed for the city. I was *amazed* that they would have this kind of man as mayor.

I'm not amazed any longer because the one we have now is just about the same type. They both reflect the extreme conservative view of Watertown."

Al Kromholz said, "When we went to visit the Mayor, Pastor Siferd and myself, we went to try to dialogue about open housing and why the clergymen had signed a newspaper advertisement supporting open housing in Watertown. And — two things. One, I believe at that time the Mayor either called me a Communist or intimated I was a Communist. And also had the Chief of Police present, Mann, present for that meeting, as he explained to Glen Siferd, because I was a dangerous person who was prone to lie.

"Chief Mann told me privately after the meeting, some time after, that he was most embarrassed, that he had been called in by the Mayor and that he really didn't know why he was there. I don't know if that's true or not. I'm willing to believe what Chief Mann says. The Mayor, on the other hand, I felt — felt very much in control of the situation. He was by no means intent upon dialoguing with us, but I think he was very sure that he had the community opinion behind him, as well as the police powers."

Chief Mann said, "I remember being there. I can't remember what—I remember being there. For me, it was a very short meeting. I mean there was nothing to it."

I asked if the Mayor lost his temper.

"There was no losing of temper or anything," Mann said. "I mean, I'm trying to think what all transpired there, there was nothing out of line. The reason the Mayor called me, I didn't know anything about this meeting, the Mayor called me and this meeting was supposed to have been with Kromholz. Alone. And of course he brought this Siferd along with him. And the Mayor of course didn't want to be outnumbered or to be misquoted on anything so he called me on the phone and asked if I would come over. And I didn't know what it was about until I came over there and he told me he had an appointment with Kromholz to discuss — I can't even remember what they were going to discuss, to be honest with you. Like I said, it's been a number of years ago. I can't truthfully remember what all transpired but I mean there was no —"

I interrupted, You don't remember the Mayor losing his temper?

"No, he definitely — no," Mann said. "He didn't lose his temper. No. Absolutely no. For the life of me I can't remember what this meeting was about."

I asked Mann to verify if in fact he had told Alan Kromholz quite awhile after this meeting that he was embarrassed to be there, didn't really know why he was there.

Mann replied, "Well — I mean this. Again, there's nothing worse than getting in the middle of something. See, I wasn't taking sides with the — this is one thing that you have to know about law enforcement. I wasn't about to be put in the middle of something, and this is what happened. As I say, I was not aware of the fact that this meeting was taking place. So I was called over the phone and suddenly I'm in the middle of a little — conflagration there, that I didn't want to get in."

So what Kromholz said was correct?

"Yes," Mann said. "I mean you'd be embarrassed too in a situation like this."

Mike Bentzin said, "Then Kromholz asked for an appointment about guns, civil rights, open housing and what all. He didn't tell me he'd bring Siferd, who was new in town and didn't know what was going on, so I told Pecky [Chief Mann's nickname] to be there. This's after he'd gotten off the pulpit that Sunday and ran up and down the aisle challenging the congregation, and said he was always going to be an activist.

"Anyway, so there was this meeting he wanted to have in my office, so he started out and I said, 'You be quiet! Now I'm gonna do what you did to me in church two or three weeks ago.' Everyone in town heard about it of course. When they came in, see, there's two doors, big wooden doors. One here [pointing with his left hand] and one here [pointing with his right hand] and eveyone knew what was going to happen and so they were all listening at the doors. And I gave him the devil for marching and what all and Siferd after awhile looked at him and said, 'I think this man has a vendetta. We're not gonna get anywhere. Let's leave.' And Pecky said, 'That's right, you're not going to get anywhere.' I gave him the devil and you know what, he put out his hand and thanked me for the appointment! And the next day, he was in the post office with two other guys and I didn't even see him and I was talking with one of the guys he was with and he said, 'Well, hello, Mayor, how are you? as if nothing had happened! I mean it really was something!

"And people then kept calling me up and saying, 'That was good, Mike. Time someone told him off!'"

Soul

I

In the beginning of November *Soul*, *"one of the underground,"* was published. It consisted of two sheets of paper stapled together and mimeographed on four sides. It was anonymous and contained a number of typographical errors. *Soul* quickly created a furore in town and its distribution was widely enlarged when copies were run off by officials in the City Hall. Although the magazine ran for four issues, only the first two created controversy, and of these the first had far greater impact on the community. *Soul* proved to be one of the most controversial elements of Alan Kromholz's ministry.

The magazine grew out of a senior high school discussion group led by Kromholz. The group itself was not an innovation of his; the former minister, Steve Evans, had started such a group. From the beginning of Kromholz's ministry the group met at 6:45 a.m. on Fridays. In the fall the group named itself the Youth Strategy Movement and soon became centered around *Soul*. One member of the group, Scott Pauli, said, "It wasn't a movement with a publication; it was a publication with a group." There were some six to eight high school students who were regularly involved in the beginning of *Soul*; by the end of the school year there were some fifteen involved in one way or another. Not all of those involved, even of the core group, were from the Congregational Church.

Sydney McQuoid, the daughter of Weir and Vivian McQuoid, was deeply involved in the publication of *Soul*. Like most of those involved, Syd was a junior in high school. During the summer of 1967 she had participated in a Milwaukee Ecumenical Inner Core Seminar where she came in contact with Father Groppi and the NAACP Youth Council. "I had just been in the ghetto," she said, "and although I'd driven through it before I hadn't really lived with these people and really talked with them. And found out the lack of communication between small towns and big cities, and the misconceptions that the media give about Father Groppi. I saw scads and scads of prejudice when I was with black people, directed at them, and at me too, and it really hurt. Really a lot, you know. I wanted to do something about it; I guess I wanted to wake people up and make them aware. I wanted to change them, I think I felt I might have a chance at changing them. And if nothing else, at least wake them up so they were aware of what was happening outside the boundaries of Watertown and the Rock River."

Sydney remembered the immediate situation that led to the publication of *Soul*. She and a friend, Kathy Smith, were editors of the editorial page of the high school newspaper, *hi-scribbler*, and they became interested in writing about national and town issues, not just about dress code. Their advisor was not happy with this; they would generally write their articles anyway and tell him that he wouldn't get in any trouble, that they would take the blame. "So for a lot of things like on Vietnam and starvation and black-and-white relations, it was pretty good," Syd said. "And then we devised this thing about sex."

Syd and Kathy thought there was a real need for sex education and they devised a questionnaire which they were going to distribute. On the basis of the response they were going to write an editorial. They thought they had a pretty good idea of how the results would turn out and then they would write asking that a sex education course be established. They devised the questionnaire, and wanted to pass it out and ask for no names at all. They took it down to the principal's office.

"And he got *really* really upset and he thought we were trying to delve into everybody's personal life," Sydney said. "He felt just *astonished* that we'd ask anybody if they were a virgin or not. He just got really really upset and at the end we were talking about, well, we just feel it would be a good idea to get these things out in the open and try and get people to realize how bad this education is. And he just could *not* see it and he just got *really* upset and he ended — he was cleaning his rifle. I'll never forget that.

"He was cleaning his *rifle* and he was getting *really* mad and oh, we were sitting there scared. See, it was hunting season. And I don't know how it got there but it scared the devil out of us. We knew he wouldn't do anything but just the idea that it was there.

"Then he said, 'Well, I'm *glad* — Kathy how old are you? Seventeen? — that you think that you're so *knowledgeable* on these subjects,' 'cause I guess she was saying with more information on the topic, things might decrease. And he got very defensive and very slanderizing, more or less, on our character, when we had no idea we would go in and talk about this.

"And so, after that we got really frustrated, and we went and told our frustrations to this group, the Youth Strategy Movement, and we just thought, well, wouldn't it be a good idea to start an underground newspaper? Al really didn't have that much to do with it. He didn't bring up the idea for a newspaper at all. We thought, well, we'll write our own newspaper and we thought we'll call it an underground newspaper because it's not sanctioned by anything. I think I was the one that brought it up, and my mother had suggested, 'Well, why don't you write your own?' He [Kromholz] liked the idea and encouraged us to go on. And we chipped in our own money and got donations from other people."

I asked if they had given any thought to signing the articles.

"Yeah," Syd said, "we thought, we thought very much, the first page we really thought about signing it. We didn't think it would be such an outrage because we were going to go and distribute them and we were going to acknowledge, if anybody asked who had written it, we would say. So we didn't think it would matter so much in our paper but we were just afraid if it was *written* down, we were afraid — you see there were a lot of kids coming up for scholarships and it was for the next year and it was really important, and recommendations for college, and we were afraid that if he [the school principal] had gotten hold of this with the proof of our names, that he would just slanderize us, that he would just really — we were afraid of that. Well, we didn't realize the commotion it would cause. We would have signed it.

"We didn't really expect a reaction, we thought they'd just say, 'Oh this is a bunch of stupid kids writing something and they don't know what they're talking about.' But instead the town got really upset."

Had they thought about toning down the articles?

"No," Sydney McQuoid said. "We thought they were kind of mild in fact."

Public Opinion: Soul
"*Soul?* Well the town was highly incensed. And then we found out it was done in the church and a lot of the kids, most of the kids, weren't even from our church. The first one [issue] got after Richards [the high school principal] and said they were spied on in restrooms." He laughed. "And it was really libelous and if they hadn't been kids they would have really been in trouble for that. The town was in quite an uproar over it. Do you know

the Senns? Well, they're staunch Baptists I think. They called me and said the kids had always been good kids but now Kromholz got hold of them and told them not to listen to their parents. They said now their kids were impossible.

He was trying to undermine. He must have been trying to deliberately ruin the church. As soon as he left, it [Soul] died a natural death. See, he was writing most of this stuff. Oh no, not the kids at all. Kromholz had written most of the first Soul. That's generally conceded."

Mike Bentzin

"This was teaching disrespect to the teachers, to the parents. I mean there were articles, don't obey your parents, don't obey the teachers, ridiculing the teachers. I don't care if they want to make statements about the police department, or law enforcement, or the politicians in town, I mean let 'em, but when they start ridiculing teaching, I think that somewhere along the line — We did have adults editing this paper, approving these articles. I don't think this is right at all."

Marlyn Mann

"The thing that I did feel in talking to people, that he would get these kids, I mean he would tell them they don't need to do what their parents say, they should do what *they* say. And this caused, I think, among people I knew, quite a bit of dissension in families. Because who's this young pipsqueak to tell the kids, pay no attention to what your parents say?"

Peg Buckland

"It could have been a fine thing. After all, it was written by a group of I would say intelligent young people, but I don't think they were the most worldly in the world. And some of the things they put in the paper had a very bad effect for the program they were actually trying to foster, and that was to be able to express themselves. The understanding I had was, he [Kromholz] read these papers before they were printed and condoned them see? I think the individual who had edited it could have gotten across the same meaning without alienating people they were talking about."

Bob Bertling

"I was more upset than Bob. I thought, *Gee,* because they wrote nasty things about parents and teachers."

Jean Bertling

"I really didn't pay too much attention to it. Every time I saw a copy I read it, but it was involved a lot with the public school, and I'm a great believer in — I think all people speak out or write what they think. I think it's a great safety valve and I was for it. I didn't care. I didn't particularly want to see any minister of ours — let's see — directly connected with it. I feel that a couple of ministers would have been fine to be on the editorial board, but as far as the paper goes, I think it was anonymous actually, I thought it was a fine thing."

Chuck Yeomans

"I was at Marge's house [Yeomans] for coffee one morning and Chuck burst into the room with mimeographed copies of *Soul.* He couldn't say a word. He just waved them and sputtered around and asked if we'd seen this trash that some of these people are putting out. And I acted very innocent like I didn't know anything about it. The very first issue, copies that they had xeroxed off at City Hall and it looked much better because they only used one side of the paper. He started criticizing them article by article and talked about how disrespectful they were being to the adults. Especially the Adult article irritated him. Soon, I guess, he gathered the impression I didn't disapprove of them an awful lot, and he sort of walked out of the room."

What did his wife think of it?

"Marge asked me if I'd like some more coffee."

Kathy Isaacson

Soul contained:

an exhortation to build up a teen coffee house,

three quotations under the heading "INVOLVE-MENT,"

"Almost everything that is great has been done by youth."

Benjamin Disraeli

"If you do not think about the future, you cannot have one."

John Galsworthy

"Taking a new step, uttering a new word, is what people fear most."

Fyodor Dostoevsky

a reiteration of the state open housing law in Wisconsin and the statement that it only covers twenty-five percent of housing,

the following generality:

"A GENERALITY—

A conspicuous thing about a NIGGER HATER:
he sure has a warped
SENSE OF VALUES.

Do you?

I laugh at him!"

Soul also had the following three titled articles:

Open Your Eyes

High school is a supposedly "higher institution of learning" and students should learn the facts of every part of life from it. But one of the most important things a person can learn is discouraged in public high schools. That is, thinking for oneself, and voicing those thoughts freely.

An education is not complete if the student has not run into opposition in ideas and opinions. But to have opposition, one has to have ideas in the beginning, yes? Stifling a teenager's natural impulse to philosophize and decide on issues is actually discouraging education. If students are used to rebukes instead of congratulation, from teachers and administrators, they are more likely to feel apathetic about it, and apathy quickly becomes a habit.

Teachers and administrators on the whole feel that free-thinking has no place in school may feel it easier to handle students that follow rather than lead. But what happens to those students when it's their turn to lead? Is it a school's right to deprive a person of developing good leadership abilities because they don't want any trouble?

An education staff should educate — not ban their students.

What other place could give facts as objectively and truthfully (hopefully) than a school? If the administration is worried about the thoughts creating an anti-everything movement, there would be less of a chance if those thoughts came from school rather than from bigoted, ignorant outsiders.

It would be quite ironic if the time came for the educators to depend upon the students they created, only to find they cannot think for themselves and need to follow the leaders that ARE NO MORE!

Spies, Spies, Everywhere!

You are a teenager. You are not to be trusted. You are forced into school at a very early age, told what you will do, when you will eat, when you will go to the bathroom, what you will wear, what you will think. Spies are placed in the bathrooms, in the bleachers, at pep assemblies, in the halls. Two-way P.A. systems are used to eavesdrop on classrooms, monitors are placed in the halls to keep you in line; passes are issued to keep you in your place. You're made to cut your hair, conforming with the rules of bald administrators. Your student newspaper is rigorously censored. All controversy is squashed. Your student council engages in meaningless campaigns and elections for a student government that is concerned mainly with trivia like whether to allow the Student Senate to vote or making Homecoming rules. The empty formal democracy of WHS is not only a frustrating experience, it has become the training ground for the acceptance of the false-democracy in which political machines determine the choices presented to the voters, and a willful executive can ruin the Constitution by turning the legislature into a rubber-stamp body.

Here we see the pathos of repression of the young, by adults who themselves are without power in the real world — without power in the corporation that employs them, in the governments that make war and collect taxes, in the school board that dictates the shape of young minds. The same adults that resent assumptions by the young that they can run their lives, that they can avoid impotence. Father knows best, damn it. But there is hope — settle into a comfortable niche in the system and become a "little box" on the hillside. The son who defies authority shows up the weakness of his father and must be taught a lesson — that passivity is "survival."

Hey, Mr. Adult!

I find that of all the articles I have ever written, those concerning civil rights are by far the hardest to compose. The reason for this is quite simple and outright. How many times can you tell a person that men are equal in the eyes of God? Those toward whom this statement is directed couldn't care less about it. They are so stuck in their ways and beliefs that they can't even seem to understand that the only difference between us and the Negro is a little bit of pigment. You have pigment too, white brother. It's just pink. But people, especially the adults in Watertown, are too close-minded to accept the realistic facts. This is evident not only in the civil rights issues, but also in the consensus concerning education and culture in Watertown. This town is very culturally deprived, and it's due to the people who live here. People here also seem to fail to realize the importance of high quality education.

Such education depends upon good resources. Recall, Mr. ADULT, all the trouble Watertown had in building a Junior High School with highly developed facilities. Thank you, Mr. ADULT, for being so hearty at giving your youth such a wonderful chance.

But we the youth have something over you Mr. ADULT. We're progressive, open minded, and on the move. We hold nothing against the Negro because he has different pigment (such a trivial matter to argue!). Rather we're striving to develop ourselves into well rounded persons with open minded attitudes. We're striving to stay out of the local egotistical mindset into which many of you wonderful ADULTS have fallen. The world calls for change. Change calls for involvement.

We have realized that you will never change your long indoctrinated egotistical attitudes. So we the youth have taken our stand, but many of us find that you the ADULT won't even allow this. I know of several cases where a son or daughter has wanted to take a stand on civil rights, even in so much as marching in Milwaukee, and the parents, uninvolved themselves, would not allow their child to his own opinion, and enforced this unreasonable dictatorship with an invitation for the youth to pack up and leave. In such cases, we the youth, must realize and obey your ruling. But deep inside, Daddy, we're right. We know that you the ADULT will never give the Negro a chance. But you will die. And then WE will give him what he is entitled.

I I

Sydney McQuoid told me that *Soul* became the main focal point of her whole life during her junior year. "It just developed totally and my whole life revolved around it. In a way, after awhile, it had to because a lot of my social problems came up because of my involvement. Parents were leery of having their kids associate with me. I told you about that one guy that couldn't date me because of that — I was going out with him in the beginning of the year and his mother found out that I was in *Soul* and she didn't want him to have anything to do with me because he might get connected with it. And there were also vicious rumors going around about me being pregnant. Of course, sex always has to come into it even though it has *nothing* to do with it.

"I felt quite alienated a lot of the time. I felt whenever I was walking down the street that people were very conscious of me and I guess, well, very stand-offish. Even a bit of fear and hatred because of what I did. And also I depended on my family a lot more because we did a lot more together. We were sort of forced to maintain a relationship that was always open and forgiving of things because of this closeness."

It made your family closer?

"Yeah," Sydney said, "not only because of the necessary openness but — well, my father's job was sort of threatened and we had to take a stand together. My father had gotten sort of inklings — he didn't really think he would get fired, there were just inklings in the air that something might happen.

"So, we sat down one night, my father, mother, and I, and discussed this, and I had to decide if it was important to me to go to a private school which would cost a lot more than just going to a state university. And with the money situation if it happened that he would get fired. And we decided that this was more important, our stand here, was a lot more important to us and to the community and to the world than whether or not I went to a so-called elite college. And so we took the stand together, and he wasn't fired or anything, but — "

Why was the response so fierce against the magazine?

"I often wonder about that," she said. "I think it probably was because we were challenging something that was so dear to them and that they had grown up with. Well, we were challenging their whole life style, everything they believed in, everything they lived for. The whole idea, especially with the civil rights thing, the whole idea that you have to work for what you get out of life. And this is a big thing around here that you have to work for what you get."

Why did you decide to go ahead and shake up these peoples' realities?

"Because we felt it was very necessary that they, and that we too, look at what is going on and related to the poverty situation and the civil rights situation because most of us will enter urban areas and be faced with this and even if the people aren't going to go into urban areas, still it involves all humans and we just have to face this because our country is very bound up in it. Community is not just Watertown, and that was the main trouble, because most people felt that the community ended outside of the city limits. Their responsibility was only toward the city, toward their family. It wasn't to, say, the outer world unless, say, their sons got drafted. But really community extends to the whole world."

I asked what she thought of Al Kromholz's whole tactic of open confrontation.

"I liked it," Sydney said. "I respect him very much. Because I've always felt there are a lot of people that are really really hypocritical that would hide behind themselves and never confront an issue, not even take sides, but really look at it and then decide what they're going to do about it. These things are terribly important, they have to decide if it's important to them. I thought that was the only way that could bring it out in the open. That could really get people concerned about it."

You don't think he could have gotten more done with a milder manner?

"No, because people didn't even think there was a problem. People didn't even think there was anything to be dissatisfied about. If people don't think that, how can you persuade them? You can't. You have to hit it to them. I guess you have to bring out their fears and that's what we did. Inside. I think people have been hiding them for an awful long time.

"Sometimes I wished he'd hit a little stronger in his sermons. He got hung up on theological stuff and it kind of dragged it out. He really toned down his sermons, I think. Like they were nothing compared to some of our raps we had on violence. He really hit us at Youth Strategy Movement. We discussed lots of things that would never come up in his sermons. We discussed the marches and what would happen if they'd turn to violence. And would it be good if they turned to violence? And the whole radical movement to violence? He had us convinced he *could* be violent if the situation called for it. And you know, I was sixteen and a junior in high school and — And about resisting the draft and going to Canada. If he'd even said anything about going to Canada, people would have really — just really been upset. In a way, people could say we were expressing his views, but they were ours first and then we realized we agreed."

During this time did you ever question why Al was doing this or his wisdom?

"There was no time that us kids got together to purposely discuss that. It was funny because you see Al wasn't there a lot of the time when we were writing up *Soul.* In fact, he had *nothing* to do with the first issue. Nothing. He did not write any articles. I think he went along with the idea, thought it was a good idea but — and that was another thing too that people accused him of writing the whole issue but he, in fact, he read it while he was mimeographing it. It was wonderful too that he trusted us so much. That he was allowing us to speak out and — I'll admit there were probably some discrepancies in *Soul,* and that we made mistakes along the way in the way we handled a lot of things. And the fact that he trusted us and allowed us to make all these mistakes was very—" Sydney was speaking very quietly now, "moving, for us."

One particularly memorable event in November for Sydney was when she received a phone call. "The phone call was a Tuesday night and it was — the middle of November. That was really a traumatic experience because my little sister *could* have answered the phone. Jaynie got up to get it and I said, 'Oh, I'll get it 'cause I thought it was for me 'cause it usually is. First of all he said, 'Is this the mother of the girl that's involved in *Soul*?'

"And I said, 'No, this is the daughter.'

"And he said, 'Oh, you.' He says, 'Why don't you stick to your own business, you nigger lover, why don't you go off and marry a nigger? Why don't you just get out of town?'

"And I was just really upset. It was an older man, I remember, older than my father. I remember I was just really upset and I started crying. And he had just said those three things and then I hung up and he was gonna go on or something. And he didn't even know if it was me, the daughter that had done it. It could have been my little sister.

"My mother came running in. I thought I had hung up real nicely but I guess I'd slammed it down. She came in and she wondered what was wrong and I talked to her about it. So then we called Ruth, 'cause we'd known she'd gotten a lot of these phone calls and we talked to her about it. And then I guess my dad went over to talk to Ruth or something, 'cause she was really upset that *I* had gotten one.

"And then two other times after that I got two phone calls, or three phone calls on the same night and I answered and there was just someone breathing. They didn't say anything for about two minutes. This was about the week after. And then the third time my father answered the phone and said, 'Listen, this call's traced.' So he never called again."

Speaking more generally, Sydney McQuoid said, "Something's gotta happen. I mean it's just *gotta*. And I suppose we've been saying that for so long and it seems like with the Vietnam War and the black situation and everything, it's not getting better and it doesn't seem like anyone's really concerned about it, *less* concerned than during the time of *Soul*. And now with this Black Panther thing, with the police raids on the Black Panthers, and it looks like it was just the police, and with Nixon appeasing people with his minimum withdrawals, it seems so hopeless because even with the big march in Washington with the moratorium [November 15, 1969] it's just a very dim outlook. I can't see that there's going to be any change and I feel very definitely there has to be. And — as far as I'm concerned, let the Revolution come.

"And I wonder if I'm just going to end up being — liberal. Even though how great my parents are, I still don't want to be like them. And I don't have any alternative really. Sometimes I feel like junk the whole thing and just forget it, leave it, it's such a mess you can't do anything anyway. Just forget it. In a way I feel that going to college is junking the whole thing. And I don't like that. But, uh — "

III

I talked with Donovan Richards, the principal of Watertown High School. Richards, a former athlete, is in his late thirties, and is not a member of the Congregational Church.

I asked him what the response of the town had been to *Soul*.

"I felt at the time that it came out, personally, I was bothered about it because of the approach," he said. "The first one that came out was very poorly done, poor taste, and a lot of unsigned articles, and things like that. But personally I was kind of, I was upset about it and concerned about it. But I felt this way about it as far as the school is concerned: that as long as this was not printed here, and it was not distributed here in school, that even though as a school official, and myself personally I was concerned about it, that I would not take it upon myself, the principal of the school, to try and do something about it. In one way it was kind of — none of my business.

"I think the main effect of it was at that time, as I recall, is that other youth kind of just put it down, as not being interested in it. They either disagreed with it or the type of material in it they just didn't like."

We went through the first issue of *Soul,* article by article. I asked Donovan Richards if he could point out a few things that upset people. I asked if people were offended by the term "a nigger hater."

"I would say so, yes," he said. "This kind of approach, when those kinds of words and terms are used, when you talk about the 'nigger hater,' 'bigots' and 'hypocrites,' those kind of terms are the things that aggravate people. For those kinds of causes it appears to me that when you go about them so that you put somebody on the defensive by what you say and the way you do it, you hurt your cause rather than help it.

"Here where it talks about institutions of higher learning and so forth, I think part of the thing here is that it's just a misinterpretation of what a high school is. Like 'is a supposedly higher institution of learning that persons can learn is discouraged and that the most important things people can learn in school is discouraged, thinking for oneself and voicing those thoughts freely.' That's just not true. School just doesn't operate that way. This statement that 'thinking for oneself and voicing your thoughts and individual freedom and critical thinking are discouraged' just isn't true. Now I'm *sure* that our teachers would tell you that one of the things that they really have is so-called freedom to teach. Now naturally we have a course of study and certain things that we want to have covered, say in a U.S. history course, but as far as this being structured so that it's a brain-washing situation, indoctrination, it just isn't true. I think that this [the article] is a radical approach to this.

" 'You're so used to rebukes instead of congratulations, from teachers and administrators, they are more likely to feel apathetic about it, and apathy quickly becomes a habit.' Again, it just isn't true. Here, 'Teachers and administrators on the whole feel that free-thinking has no place in school may feel it easier to handle students that follow rather than lead.' Again, it just isn't, it just plain is not true.

"And this about spies, spies everywhere, in the bathroom, the two way P.A. system, in the halls, in assemblies, this. Sure, we have a two-way P.A. system but that P.A. system has *never* in the history of the school been used to even listen on a *teacher's* classroom. It has nothing to do with the student. It's two-way in that you can make announcements to the classrooms, and there is a communication system on it so that if the football coach is in the gym and he has a phone call we can say down, 'Is Mr. McQuoid there?' 'Yes.' 'Well could you please come to the high school office, you have a phone call.'"

I said, They say something about dress codes —

Richards read, " 'You're made to cut your hair conforming with the rules of bald administrators.' We do have dress codes at the present time. Since this was written our dress code has changed considerably, it has been liberalized quite a bit since this was written."

As a result of that?

"No. At the time this was written one of the things that had not taken place is that through the Student Council and through the students, they had not made a definite proposal for changes in the dress code. And one of the things we said that we were going to insist on in changing the dress code is that it be incorporated into it as how and where would students accept responsibility to go along with the guideline and show where they would be responsible."

At the present time can girls wear slacks to school?

"No, they cannot."

What would happen if there weren't any dress code?

"I really don't know for sure," Donovan Richards said. "I do not think that I could honestly say that if we did not have a dress code, that it would affect the learning that takes place in school. I really don't think I could honestly say that."

Do a lot of people feel that it would?

"Some people certainly do. Some staff members certainly do and some of the administrative staff certainly does, but I do not really think that I could say that. I think I'm more liberal on it than I was. I wouldn't say two years ago but certainly five years ago. Another thing I feel about the dress code is I think it's good for students, as an educational experience, that there are some standards of dress and appearance that they're required to meet. I have to, the butcher downtown, the waitress, the people who work in the shoe factory, the mechanics in the garage, it's different for them but their employers do say, 'Your appearance shall be like this' and in that sense I think it's a good learning experience. That's one of the kinds of things they're going to have to meet in society, and if by having something in school that we can help them get used to this — that's kind of like good attendance. People are very concerned that the people they employ have good attendance, and of course, this is something that we try to stress.

"I would like to see students, you know they talk about being concerned about student welfare, things like that, and the thing that ninety-nine and nine tenths percent of it centers on is things like dress code, student lounge, senior privileges, breaks, open campus, these types of things — I would think that students could make a real contribution to the welfare of students, and they, I believe, are in the best position to do so, if they would really work together, and do things to help each other, in such things as drinking, use of drugs, morals, use of the automobile, real things like this where they could really help each other."

I asked if kids wouldn't want to drink if their parents do.

"Yes, I think that's very true. Again, it comes back

to a matter of law. But I can see certainly why they would want to. Most of the time that they're drinking it's going to involve being with other groups where the effects of the drinking, such as a breakdown in morals, driving, things like this, are almost required. Something like driving, we kill thousands and thousands of people on the highways and I just don't see youth protesting drinking and driving. I asked Student Council, if nothing else, at least make a statement that you support Governor Knowles' ten-point program for reducing traffic fatalities."

I asked if there was anything else I should know about this. I said I couldn't think of any more questions.

"I don't think so," Richards said. "I personally feel that Reverend Kromholz was wrong in his radical approach in what he tried to do. Personally, I wouldn't question his genuine sincerity, interest in the cause and so forth, but the method that he used I think was wrong, the radical approach, and I think that at the time he was doing it, he devoted too much of his time to it and it almost became a phobia with him, and that other things in the church, other responsibilities of his job that he just didn't do. That's my observation."

You criticized his methods. Do you think that basically what he wanted was a good thing?

"Well, I wouldn't for one minute question that his goal wasn't to make this world a better place, just plain more consideration for fellow human beings, and sure this involves tolerance of the Negro, of the Spanish American, of each other."

IV

Donovan Richards gave me the name of the daughter of friends, who, he said, expressed the majority student opinion of *Soul*. The friends were Frank and Pat van der Hoogt. The van der Hoogt's daughter, Barbara, was a senior in high school when *Soul* was published.

"Well, first of all I had a prejudice against the church," Barb said. "I was not in the church in any way, in any form. It was the kind of thing where I got to be a certain age and I said I'm not going to church. And Mom and Dad would say, well, you really *should* go to church, and this is when we were about twelve, around that age. And so we'd fight whether we had to go to church or not. It was the thing to do, to fight not to go to church. As it turned out, we went to church for awhile and then we just sort of dropped off when this thing started. It was mainly because my parents dropped off that we dropped off.

"And at that time I was into the high school life very much. I was in sort of a cliquish group, this type of thing. I don't think I was ready to get involved in anything quite this — I don't want to call it dramatic — but you know, anything like this because I'd been living in Watertown, and I've changed a lot since then and I can see some merit in it now but at that time I was into being leaders of clubs and in Student Council, AFS, this sort of thing. I was very involved with school and I knew all the teachers and this sort of thing. I worked hard — in high school — which is very different from now."

Speaking of *Soul*, Barb said, "Well, it said some pretty strange things, to a Watertown person. And I read them and thought, I was sort of blasé about the whole thing, I didn't really look at them as good or bad. In fact, I sort of liked the poetry and stuff in them but I never really involved myself to evaluate it."

Were you horrified at it?

"Oh no. No no no."

Do you remember the reaction of the kids in the high school at the time?

"Well the whole thing is, it wasn't just the *Soul* magazine, it was all the little things behind it that people reacted to. First of all, I would say that many many of the people in the high school were into what high school people are, which is what I was into.

"Like Kathy Smith, and Syd, and some of these people, I don't know quite how they got into something else. But anyway, they were just a little bit further left than we were, so to say. As far as the high school, it really didn't make much of any impression on anybody, I never heard it discussed very much. I think it was discussed a lot within the people that did the magazine. Also there were a couple of people that were helping with the magazine, David Schultz was one of them, well, I have *never* gotten along with David Schultz, and my personal feelings toward him, I think, and how *he* discussed the magazine, just completely turned me off and I thought well, forget it. I don't look at the merit, I looked more at the merits of the people behind it, that were pushing it, rather than I did just entirely the magazine. I think I was right in doing that too because they were the ones that were writing it so I was seeing their ideas.

"As far as Kromholz goes, I don't know. First of all, I don't know how it happened, but I've always had this very standoffish sort of thing with any sort of minister and that was one thing. He just always seemed to me, the impression I got from meeting him the first time is that he was trying to pry into my life. And especially since he was connected with the church. Maybe I had a fear of God or something," Barb laughed, "but I don't know, I just wanted absolutely nothing to do with him. I think I was a little bit frightened of him in a way. I don't know, his appearance somehow frightened me a little. Just the way he talked, he seemed to talk very smoothly like he really knew what he was talking about. I don't know, I just *never* could get together with him as a person at all.

"And his sermons — I think that if I heard his sermons and didn't think of him as Kromholz, as I knew him, I think I'd think that they were good sermons, but not appropriate to give in the Watertown, this Congregational Church. I mean there's such a thing as being progressive but I don't know, I still think, well, like you can have so much violence and it's going to set things back rather than set them forward. And I just think he went a little too quickly and was a little bit too powerful in speaking and I think he sort of towered over the people of the congregation as sort of a lord and master and telling them what to do rather than accepting them as equals. And a little group formed around him consisting of these kids who really dug him. It was a strange sort of separation because I wasn't on either side really but — I think there were quite a few people who weren't on either side."

Discussing sermons, Barb said, "He was giving some sermon on the racial problems or something and he said we ought to start bussing blacks into Watertown. I mean this completely *freaked* people. Can you imagine these people in Watertown, all these *blacks* running around, I mean — And I don't know, I spent a lot of time in Milwaukee with friends who are black and when I was in high school we had a black exchange program and stuff like that and I really believe this is the best way to go about it. I mean, we brought our black friends to the town and people would give us sort of strange looks, there was some prejudice around but it wasn't quite as stiff as somebody getting up and yelling, we ought to bus the blacks in. Even if we're not doing it.

"He just somehow couldn't get together with the type of people in Watertown. And I think that maybe in a different situation I would have thought him an admirable man. Because I think he was very dedicated but he was also very emotional and very strong and he wanted this and this and this done but he just couldn't get together with the idea that the people in Watertown couldn't do it that way. It was impossible according to their backgrounds and everything else."

I asked what she thinks of her parents' political views at this point.

"Well, my mother isn't really together with politics," Barb said. "She really isn't. She's very emotional about it. We can be discussing something in somebody else's terms and she'll be very logical but to discuss it in my terms, it blows up. My dad can discuss it logically either way. And it's very strange, I really think that my dad's political views are basically very sound and I don't think they're Republican, I don't think they're Democrat, I think he's a sort of a very strange combination of different things. I think of any man I've ever met, I admire his values the most, that I've ever met, because he may be a businessman but just some of the things he's done in his life, just his idea of, he doesn't care at all about material things. My mother's always very worried about finances and stuff like this, and my dad doesn't make good money and he doesn't care. He's just perfectly happy with what he's doing. He doesn't have his closet full of suits, he's got two suits and he doesn't care. It's sort of opposition to what he believes. I don't know, I don't know, I can't really say what I think of his political views. I just admire him completely."

What does your father think of draft dodgers and draft resistance?

"I'm not quite sure," she said. "He was in the Air Force. I don't think he respects them very much. I do. I think that's one of the places we differ the most. It's the whole thing about America. I'm a lot more pessimistic than I was about it and I think the government's a big screw and nobody knows what's happening."

Your father doesn't think that?

"No. He's basically very optimistic. He thinks something's the matter with the government but he thinks everything should be done through politics, voting. He said why are those kids screaming over there? He said all those kids that don't vote. Do you know what the voting percentage was here and there? He's right in a way but see, I just don't believe it can be done that way anymore."

Does he think that if poor people work hard they can work themselves out of poverty?

"Yeah."

Do you think that?

"No, I don't," Barb van der Hoogt said. "I don't think America is what it used to be."

Scott Pauli, a congregation member, was a junior in high school when he was actively involved in *Soul*. "It was really hard on me because up until that time, I was the all-American kid type thing," Scott said. "Like I got the God and Country Award in Boy Scouts. It's really the hardest award. It's allegedly more difficult to attain than an Eagle Scout, which is not too easy. It takes a year of study with the minister of the church once a week and you do projects and you do a lot of religious study, and then you get this big award and it's given in the church in front of the congregation during a service. So I was really the all-American kid in the church, the Good Guy, and then this whole thing came up and people started to change their minds about me, and like, it bothered me.

"It upset quite a few teachers that had thought quite a lot of me before-hand and were rather hesitant — and then of course most of them just passed it off as 'Well the kid's just going through this, making a few mistakes, he doesn't really realize what he's doing. I guess the kid's still okay. It's Kromholz.'

"I think the people in this town are sheltered enough that they think kids are all good. Even when *Soul* came out, I think more people blamed this on Kromholz than anyone else. Like we were being misled, misguided, and he was using us."

Is that true? I asked.

"No," Scott said. "But like people couldn't believe that. He had little influence at all, he just kinda kept the spirit going. People figured, oh, he was in there, the Commie ruining us all. And people couldn't believe, well, like Sydney and I were doing pretty well in school, most of us were — in fact, all of us were, and like we were honor roll kids and they just couldn't believe we'd pull something so deviant. So they blamed it all on Kromholz.

"I was very hesitant at first, I didn't march or any-thing. I didn't march when everybody else did. I didn't think it did any good and I thought it upset people very much. And I didn't think it was the way to change peoples' minds, but I've changed my mind quite a bit."

How did you start changing your mind? What caused it?

"Well, I was really a put-on," Scott said. "Like I wasn't this all-American kid that I was made out to be, that I'd been fooling people with. And I was always worried over the image bit. And like you just get out there and after awhile you see things like, even until this week I didn't believe in the selective violence thing — maybe subconsciously but I didn't know it, and then I saw this cop just beat the hell out of this kid and it just makes you sick. Slowly these things happen to you and you change. And people in Watertown don't see these things and they don't change. Specifically what I saw, I don't know."

Scott mentioned his girl friend, Ruth Richter. I had heard that her father's job was threatened because of her involvement in *Soul*, and by way of identification said, "Oh, whose father's job was threatened?"

"No," Scott said, "that's not true. He was afraid it would be. He was very very upset. She wasn't officially in it [*Soul*] but she had come to several meetings and she was there one time when the Mayor walked in and made us all leave. And the Mayor asked her who she was, and she wasn't a member of the church, so she shouldn't be there. And her father found out about this and he was very *very* upset. But his job was not really threatened, no. I guess Frater [his employer] was really in there against Al but we were really sheltered from this a lot more as kids than Al. Like Al really got the real hard stuff from these people. We were considered to be the victims of this Communist. So we really didn't get knocked as much. I think Syd got knocked more than anybody."

Did it have an effect on your life that you're aware of?

"Fantastic effect. I don't know, it really got me active in social — I don't know what. It *really* made me alive. It gave me a lot of guts I didn't have before. It made me very much aware of what certain people were really made of underneath all their coverup. Schmutzlers, and all the people who were really against Kromholz. At first people were really nice about it, like, 'Well, Pastor, we don't really feel that you should be marching,' and then as things got a little rougher and *Soul* started knocking people, people got a little — I think that if it hadn't been for *Soul*, Al would probably still be here. I really think that did it."

I asked what he thought of Al Kromholz as a minister.

"I think he's what a minister should be. He was out there to be crucified in a sense. Like I was talking to a kid who's studying to be a minister and like the kid's really out there and he's really liberal, he's really shooting away, and he told me that if you're not kicked out of your church twice in your lifetime, then you're just not doing it. And like I don't want it understood that Al was out there trying to be fired but he wasn't going to get out there and kiss somebody just to stay where he was at. He's a for-real guy. I thought he was good, a fantastic guy.

"But you know somehow I don't really think of him as a minister because the stereotyped minister is not out there fighting. I just think of him as a friend or as a real human being, a person that I really like. He's just not a minister to me. I rarely think of him as a minister."

Speaking of the total experience, Scott said, "It just made you think. Constantly. And it made you *realize* people, and it's such a great thing. Like if it wasn't for *Soul*, I wouldn't be marching on the U.W. [University of Wisconsin] campus, I have a good idea, because I'd just be afraid."

During the summer of 1970 when I talked with Scott he told me he had made some attempt to join R.O.T.C. in order to get back the II-S draft deferment he had lost when he dropped out of school. He said he had a friend in R.O.T.C. who looked into it for him. Scott said his friend "gave this Major my name and at the time they were really hard up for recruits and so the Major took it upon himself to see if I was okay. To see if I had a criminal record, grades, et cetera. My friend, Chuck, said the Major said there was some record that I had been antidraft. We figured it was because of *Soul*." Scott was referring to the last issue of *Soul* to which they had stapled a card for a Milwaukee draft counseling organization. He went on, "It was on record somewhere. We figured it was the F.B.I. but we don't know. But it was on record somewhere."

Then you don't know that you couldn't have joined?

"No," Scott said.

Why didn't you?

"I just changed my mind, man."

VI

One time I asked the Bentzins how they would describe America today.

Mike Bentzin said, "Well, I'd say it's turning to the right. It's in turmoil, as far as our younger people are concerned."

Mrs. Bentzin said, "It's confused, confused."

What is? I asked.

"The young people are confused," she replied. "When they get past elementary education they have been influenced by people who don't have the best interests of the country at heart."

Bentzin said, "The reason for the turmoil in the schools is the teachers and professors. Just because Harrington's [the former chancellor of the Madison campus of the University of Wisconsin] daughter married a colored in Chicago doesn't mean that kind of permissiveness should be on the campus. And now they've said that to him. He's got to go. And this fellow Fleming [chancellor of the Madison campus before Harrington and now president of the University of Michigan]. He was locked in here and then they arrested the kids and you know what he did? He went and bailed them out! That doesn't make any sense at all. There wasn't *any* trouble at Michigan until he went there. And now — And then there's judges like Doyle encouraging permissiveness. You do something and the judges just let you off."

Mrs. Bentzin said in her deliberate and concerned way, "I'm also very concerned about the tremendous power of the federal government, the tremendous taxing power of the federal government. And the waste. I know how poorly the dollar is spent."

Joy Bentzin told me that when she visited several military bases she saw how things would be ordered and never used. "We spend too much on the military," she said. "I can't go for the supersonic. Too expensive and unnecessary. We blow hot and cold depending on the mass media, which has been so unjust."

Mike Bentzin said, "They blow up the sensational stuff. I'm concerned about the permissiveness of parents, aside from the professors. Half the time parents don't know where their kids are."

"And drugs, kids on drugs. And pollution," Mrs. Bentzin said.

"Pollution can be taken care of," her husband replied. "We've had problems like that for a long time and I'm sure it can be taken care of. All of a sudden everyone's concerned about pollution. The press makes these fads. Under the guise of freedom of the press a lot of false things are said that shouldn't be."

Mrs. Bentzin said, "One thing that *really* really bugs me is we try to teach children to speak as ladies and gentlemen and their whole vocabulary is four-letter words. I *abhor* it. If I'm talking to someone and they say a word like that, it spoils the whole conversation for me. You'd think that's their whole vocabulary."

I asked if the turmoil due to professors and teachers is related to Communism.

"Absolutely," Mike Bentzin said. "You don't have

to have a card to be a Communist. The kids in SDS don't have cards."

Is there Communism in Watertown?

"Sure," he said. "The guy who was city attorney is an avowed atheist. And your pals up on the hill, the Isaacsons, she told me she was in SDS. 'Course that was a few years ago but look what's happened since."

Is Communism related to Russia?

"*Absolutely*," Bentzin replied. "Where do you think they get their money from? And all their information? Now this Angela Davis. She's colored but good-looking. I can see why this Poindexter would want to shack up with her. He's very wealthy, from Chicago, his wife died a few months ago. Well, his mother was a Communist. She said so, it's no secret.

"And then these do-gooders on the church board. They don't believe me when I say something but I can't be more specific since I get my information from the Police Department. We built up the Department when I was on the Commission and a lot of the guys went on the force then, and you keep up those contacts."

What do you think of the war on poverty?

"It's like pollution," Mike Bentzin said. "As long as we've been on earth we've been warring on it. But there will always be poor people. It's in the Bible. The poor will always be with us. There are people who just don't want to live like the average person. You're always gonna have it. If you put a group of people on a desert island with the same amount of money soon a few people would have most of it. It just works that way."

High Tension

I

By the first week in November tension had built up to a very high point between a large part of the congregation and their minister — tension over Kromholz marching with Father Groppi, very actively working to influence local legislation, and sponsoring the publication of *Soul*. There was also serious question about the extent to which Alan Kromholz was carrying out his pastoral duties. On September 12, at the height of Groppi's activities, a member of the congregation, Charles Graf, died. Kromholz had performed the funeral but Mrs. Graf felt he had not shown proper pastoral concern afterwards. It was a very widespread feeling that he was negligent in carrying out his pastoral duties, particularly in making sick calls. Chief Mann for example told me, "He never had time to visit. If he wants to march, that's his business. But there were people who couldn't leave their house and I know for a fact that they were never visited while he was minister. Not once."

Bill Guyer, who was the church moderator, lay leader of the congregation, remembered early November. "There was, I had the feeling at least, that antagonisms were building up," he said. "In fact, it wasn't a feeling, it was a certainty and I kept trying to get him — Kromholz — to mend these breaks, so to speak. Talked to him about meeting some of these people, calling on them, visiting with them. And he agreed with me and said in effect that he would. I think probably about the first one he called on he had a bad experience."

Who was that?

"Well, it wouldn't make much difference but anyway there was not a pleasant conversation apparently. So, he dropped it. And I came back to it again with him and at that time he started making some phone calls. And, it was too late. So some of these people said no, they wouldn't, they didn't want to meet with him. They said they would meet with him as a group. I kept discouraging the idea of any meeting because I didn't want this thing to blow this church up. I was afraid this is exactly what would happen."

The tension culminated in a meeting held on November 17. The meeting was not an official one but was held in the church alongside the sanctuary.

Al Kromholz remembered what led to the meeting. He told me that in the beginning of every November the church has a bulk solicitation drive and that this year there was grave concern expressed that the church would not be able to meet its financial obligations "because people were turning off and keeping their money, due to the activities." He told me he met with Gordon Frater, a congregation member, and at that meeting was urged by Frater and Guyer, who was also present, to meet with others individually. He said he agreed to and was able to meet with one couple, the van der Hoogts, before he called Peg Buckland. "But when I tried to arrange individual meetings with the other families, for example, Mrs. Buckland, the comment was made that I was dividing and conquering the congregation by such techniques and that I should meet with them in a large group. I wasn't concerned about that. I agreed that if they wanted to meet in a large group, fine, we would have a large group meeting. There were originally about nine families I believe which would have meant about eighteen of us getting together in the church. By the act of Mrs. Buckland many more were invited to that meeting so that fifty-five showed up."

Few people remembered the meeting in any detail. Peg Buckland for example characterized it as "just frank discussion, dialogue, back and forth. . . ."

Betty Ebert, editor of the Congregational Church's monthly newsletter, the *Church Chimes,* was one person who did remember. Mrs. Ebert is in her later fifties and is a long-time resident of Watertown. She asked me if she should just tell me the story and when I said yes, she said, "Originally I was the publicity chairman and I had to take charge of the *Church Chimes,* and I also was active in the church in the women's groups, and my circle and so forth, and one day I was down at the rummage sale and the first rumble came to me from an old elderly man, who is a member of our church and he pulled me to one side and he said, 'Say, Betty, have you heard any discontent or any rumors about our minister?'

"And I said, 'What do you mean?'

"And he said, 'Some of the men think he's so fond of the Negroes and he gets his sermons so darned full of the Negroes that the people are getting kinda tired of it, they want to hear something else.'

"This would be in the fall sometime. And I said, 'Well, he feels it very strongly, we know he's worked with the Negroes and he's a doer, and he feels it strongly.'

"And he said, 'Yeah, but here in Watertown they're getting tired of hearing it, they want to hear a little bit of the gospel and a few things like that.'

"And I said, 'Well that is the gospel, brought up to date, about the brotherhood of man and all that.'

"He says, 'Yeah, but they want to hear it right from the Bible.'

"And I said, 'Well, it's a shame there is this feeling.'

"And he said too, 'It's a shame, he's a good man and I like him, but I hear these little rumblings.'

"So then I went back and the rummage sale gals were having lunch and I said, 'I'm kinda disturbed. It's too bad but there seems to be unhappiness among the people about the minister, especially about the Negro,' and Vietnam too, that was another thing. They're all pillars of the church, from way back, and they said, 'Well I'd personally just as soon have him talk about something else,' and another one said, 'Well, he seems to be learning the hard way that that sort of thing doesn't go over in Watertown.'

"And I thought, 'Oh gee,' and so you see at that point I was simply inquiring."

Mrs. Ebert remembered when *Soul* came out. A church member called and said, " 'Have you heard about what's going on all around town? Well, you know about these kids that meet in the morning at church. Well they put out this — underground newspaper and it's hit the streets and it's *all* over town.'

"And I said, 'What's it about?'

"And she said, 'Oh it's just horrible,' and she said it just knocked down all the sacred cows of Watertown, one after the other, it just knocked them down. There's no culture in the town, the parents are narrow-minded."

I interrupted and asked if sacred cows was this woman's term.

Betty Ebert replied, "No, sacred cows is my term. I learned later that these kids had come down to City Hall with it and asked if they could spread it around. City Hall just about went through the roof.

"And no, I hadn't read it and I didn't know anything about it and I said, 'Who are these kids?'

"And she said, 'They're these kids that meet at our church. It's *our* church. I thought the minister is supposed to guide them in *loving* their mother and father, *honoring* their parents and why they certainly aren't, they're saying that the parents are a bunch of nothings.'

"And I said, 'What's a minister got to do with it?'

"And she said, 'Oh, he's their guide, he's rounding them all up and having them do it.'

"And so I thought, 'Oh boy, poor Al.'" Mrs. Ebert laughed.

"Then Joy Bentzin came over and she was telling me all about it. Oh, then I got ahold of the *Soul* and well, sure, it *was* pretty awful. It was so anonymous. I thought if the reader wanted to refute some of their allegations, you know, defend himself, where could he go to do it?

"I happened to be designing the Christmas cards for the Bentzins, I do that every year. They write out what they've been doing the last half year, and oh, they do very wonderful things, and all their kids do wonderful things, and they have me put little illustrations in the margins. And incidentally they're very good friends of ours, the Bentzins have three boys just the same age as my three boys and they all grew up together and we're all just a happy family.

"And I said, 'Oh gosh, Joy, I have to write the *Church Chimes* and I just don't know what to write, nobody's sending me any material and I know what's the big concern in the church but they just seem to want me to pretend it doesn't exist.'

"And then Joy said, 'Oh, Mike hears all about it because he's at the City Hall, and *other* ministers come and complain and they all come to Mike because he's the mayor,' and then she starts telling me all the things they were telling her. So then I said, 'Well, what does he hear?'

"And she said, 'Well, people tell him Kromholz wrote that whole paper and got it out, and the kids are nothing but patsies and giving their name to it, and he's just bringing Communism right into town through these innocent children.'

"And I said, 'Didn't the kids write it?'

"'No, and turning them against their parents and taking them down to Father Groppi, and their parents don't want them to go, and it's causing dissent in the family.'

"And I said, 'Like what?'"

"And she named one girl who she said wanted to go down to Father Groppi and march and her parents didn't want her to and she felt very badly she couldn't go and they said, 'Okay, if you go, you can pack up and leave.' So it was doing things in the home. And then she said, 'And people that are sick, he doesn't come and call on them, and people that are bereaved and somebody dies, he doesn't come and comfort them, and he's spending all his time with Father Groppi and using up the church's time.'"

"And then she said, 'And *guess* what, this *Soul* is written on the church mimeograph and our minister's helping them to *write* it. *In* our church and on church property.'"

"So then this thing was working up and working up and then Joy Bentzin would come over quite a bit and she'd call me. See, she figured I was completely on her side. I hadn't said I wasn't, all I did was ask questions.

"So anyway, all of a sudden there was this rumbling about getting him out and Joy was saying, 'To get him out we have to have a number of people, a certain majority, and there's all these rules and regulations and he really has power, he has his own supporters, there isn't any way of getting him out.'

"This was around when *Soul* came out, they were rumbling about impeachment or whatever you want to call it. I said, 'Isn't there some way we can reconcile without getting him out? He's a reasonable man and there must be some better way than that.'

" 'No,' she said, 'no, we've got to get him out.' And I still was on the fence and I hadn't completely fallen for what my daughter-in-law had written, but I have to say, she certainly had insight, expressed herself well, and she's certainly articulate."

Mrs. Ebert's daughter-in-law, a professional folk-singer, had been writing her very persuasive letters that were sympathetic to the struggle of youth in the country and in the Watertown congregation.

She continued, "So then Joy said, 'There's a meeting tonight of people, the minister has invited them.'" Mrs. Ebert told me that in fact Peggy Buckland invited them, with the help of Joy Bentzin. "And so then they all got on the phone, and I was one of them that Joy called. See, Joy didn't know, well, like I say, I was neutral. But I was awfully curious and I wanted to go just to see what cooked, especially since I had control of the publicity.

"And so I went along. I went with the Bentzins. And there we all sat. And there were fifty people. I looked around and there were fifty people of various types. There was the Mayor and his wife, and there was Peggy Buckland and her husband, and many of the old guard, of the ones who financed the church, gave nice big pledges. There weren't too many young ones, and the moderator, Bill Guyer, got up first of all and he said, 'We're all gathered here tonight for a reconciliation, a discussion, this is off the record, this is not an official meeting.' And he said, 'Even though it's not official, we would like to keep a record of it. The minister has asked me if it's all right if we have this tape recorder.'

"He had it set up, it was not on, it was set up, right there in front of everybody, and he said, 'But we'd like to get your consent to turn this on.'

"And then some of the people in the audience said, 'We don't need any record of it.'

"And the moderator said, 'Well, maybe Mr. Kromholz would like to explain that.'

"So then Mr. Kromholz got up and said, 'The reason I have this recorder here is because I've been up and down the length of Main Street recently and I have heard all kinds of quotes and misquotes and misinterpretations all having come out of my mouth for some reason or other.' And he said, 'I would like to keep the record straight because tonight I'm going to talk, and you're going to talk, and it should be on record. Just for no other reason than to later know what the record is and what I said, and what you really said. I should think you would like it for your own protection as well as mine.'

"And the audience says, 'We don't need any protection, we aren't afraid of what we're going to say. What is this meeting? Some kind of Communist thing that you have to bug it with microphones?'

"And one of the members, I *think* it was the Mayor, said, 'How do we know that you're not gonna take this whole darn tape down to WTTN and air it all over town?'

"The moderator then stepped in and said, 'We wouldn't allow it to be done. This will be strictly for our own records, for our own use, and it would be in the hands of the moderator and no one else would have access to it, and we would use it simply as a verification of what went on.'

"And they said, 'We don't need that.' *'Turn it off,'* one of the men said, *'Turn it off, pull out the plug.'* Well, it wasn't on so they didn't have to turn it off.

"Then the moderator said, 'If we're not going to have any record of it by tape, could we possibly have a written record of it? Will someone volunteer to take minutes?' In the back of the room happened to be a young girl who had just graduated with honors from the vocational school, the business college, and she said that she would do it so we settled back and relaxed and the meeting continued.

"So then the minister introduced the meeting and he said, 'I would like to hear what are the things that you are dissatisfied with? I will try to answer them. All right, does anybody want to air a complaint?'

"And I don't know in what order the complaints came but they got more preposterous as they went along. I mean a lot of them were nobody's goldarned business. One of the first ones concerned going to Father Groppi so much, 'Why are you down there all the time and why do you march with him? You are paid by the congregation and therefore you should earn your keep according to what they want you to do.'

"And a trustee got up and said, 'I just want it to be

known that the pledges have gone way down and that people aren't paying their money.'

"So then one of these people that hadn't made their pledge got up and said, 'We haven't made our pledge and we aren't paying our money and it is our way of registering a complaint.' She said, 'We're registering our dissatisfaction that we don't think we're getting our money's worth out of the church so we aren't pledging any. And we think you're spending altogether too much time down there and to the neglect of your own parish.'

"And then she said, 'We understand that Florence Grosenick was very ill over in the hospital over in Waukesha and you never came and called on her.' It so happens that he had been here only one week when she was down there.

"And he said, 'I didn't know that she was there.'

"And then, 'We understand that so-and-so's husband died, you officiated at the funeral and then you dropped her like a hot cake. And then there were all these people dying and you didn't come to their funerals or something.' It was all very anonymous, they didn't actually name the people. I thought to myself how can a church expect to have the minister punch a time clock and give a frank accounting of all the troubled souls he has helped?

"And to get on with Father Groppi they said, 'And you take the children with you, and Weir McQuoid takes those kids along down there and those kids march, and what business is it of yours to be encouraging them to do this sort of thing? That's Milwaukee's business,' and so forth.

"And he said, 'I do it because I believe in it. I do it because I can't help it, I believe in it and I think it's the only way that these colored people are going to get their desires and open housing,' and so forth, and he says, 'It's non-violent, they're simply marching, and that's why I do it.' 'But,' Kromholz says, 'I do it on my own time.'

"And they said, 'How many hours do you spend down there?'

"'Well,' he said, 'I haven't added the hours but it's strictly on my own time. I have not neglected my other duties,' and he read off, 'I have called on this many sick people — my record matches any other minister's in the church up till now, in fact, it supersedes it. And,' he said, 'this is in my spare time.'

"And they said, 'Well what spare time does a minister have?'

"And he said, 'That's a good question.' And he said, 'The children go if they want to, I don't force them. If Weir McQuoid takes his daughter down there, that's his business.' And then he just said, 'I go because I *have* to, 'cause I believe in it.'

"And of course then they tied that all in with the violence too, with the riot. And they kinda tie that in with Father Groppi and everybody. But the part that Kromholz was doing was just the marching. It's awfully hard to divide these things. And then they said, 'All right, what about all these kids that you're brainwashing? What's that all about?'

"And he said — "

Again I interrupted and asked if they used terms like that, brainwashing?

"Yeah, brainwashing, yeah. 'Course he was pretty shook but he took it very coolly and I thought he answered everybody's — these questions were coming three and four at a time, and he parried it well, I thought. And he said, 'These are young people not only of our church but of other churches. They are concerned, they are concerned about Vietnam, they're concerned about social injustice.' He said, 'After all, they're the ones that are going to have to go to Vietnam.' So he said he was a sounding board, that's all he was.

"Yeah, and then you go and let them write that stuff.'

"And he said, 'They have to express themselves.'

"And they said, 'And you write it yourself.'

"And, 'No, I didn't write it myself, I had nothing to do with the writing of it. I'm simply here as just somebody to listen to them.'

"Made sense to me, I didn't see anything terrible about that. And then they said, 'But you're turning them against their own parents and what about this kid whose parents wanted to kick her out of the house?' And I don't know what he said about that.

"And then Bentzin said, 'Do you or do you not consort with a card-carrying Communist?'

"And Kromholz said, 'I haven't ever seen his card.' " Mrs. Ebert laughed. "I thought that was real cute, 'cause they don't carry cards.

"See, there was this open housing move in town and David Fries was for it and Weir McQuoid was for it, and Kromholz was for it, and they thought a good way to add strength to it and give it momentum was to get the churches behind it. The Catholic Church succeeded, but our church didn't. So that was against him too. See, the people that were against him said that he was a rabble-rousing Communist, and the people that were for him said he had the courage of his convictions. It's all in how you look at it.

"Some of the people were trying to be reasonable with him, others were just plain hysterical. And there was this one man, he had gotten really hysterical. So every once in awhile he'd get up and say, '*I make a motion that this minister be run out of town. I don't care if we tar and feather him or on a rail, just so we can get him out of town.*'

"He said that, right there at the meeting. And I thought, boy, if that had been on a tape, that really would have been a denunciation of the audience.

"And then others were reasonable, like Neale Buckland. He's the one that withheld his pledge. He says, 'Al, you gotta face it, Al, you can't serve two masters. If you want to go down and help Father Groppi and help the Negroes, do it. Hang up your robe and go on down and do it. Or the other thing is to come here and stay with your own people and forget about Father Groppi, and serve your own community. You've got to make up your mind.' But when Neale says you can't serve two masters, in my mind, he's serving one Master who's above either one of those two. He transcends Watertown and Father Groppi.

"And oh, then Peggy got up and said, 'I understand that the young group went to Bernard Traeger, lawyer Traeger, and had a talk with him about open housing, got his viewpoint about it, and when they got done with the whole thing, one of the kids says, "You should be shot." ' And Peggy says, 'I just can't stand that kind of arrogance and sass out of young people, and you are fostering it.'

"And the minister said, 'Yes, and did you follow up on that story?'

"And she said, 'What do you mean?'

"And he said, 'Mr. Traeger forgave them and he said, "It's all right, I understand." ' So he said that lawyer Traeger was not mad at them even though they had said that. He realized they were excited.

"And then they said, 'And how about using the church mimeograph? You know darn well that the only person authorized to use it is the church secretary. And you go in there with nobody's by-your-leave, and run that thing off, and turn out that horrible newspaper. And how come you turned out that horrible newspaper without anybody's by-your-leave?'

"And he said. 'Well the facilities were here, the children had their own paper and ink, they were bound to run it off somewhere and I saw nothing wrong with it. They paid for it. The secretary's time was not paid for by the church or anything.' And he said he didn't feel he needed to get permission, after all, a minister has a little bit of power.

"They thought it was pretty awful and they said, 'You gonna do it again?'

"And he said, 'I might, they're probably going to write another one.'

"And they said, 'Well, have somebody else do it,

don't do it in our church.' And they had cleared it with Paul Jaedecke first. He was there. He was the chairman of the Board of Education. And he said that the kids had come to him and asked if they could do it before.

"And oh, Paul Jaedecke said, 'They hadn't shown us the actual copies but they had told us about what their grievances were and what they wanted to write about. But,' he said, 'they didn't clear it with me afterwards. It went to press without my having read it.'

"And then somebody said, 'We resent the anonymity of it all. Why didn't you come out and say who you were?'

"Now Kromholz admitted, he said that wasn't good. He said, 'I think they probably did it because they were scared.' And he said, 'If we turn out anymore the very front page will give the whole story, and it will say who's behind it and everything else.'"

I said that I didn't realize so much of the controversy centered around the kids.

"Yeah, *Soul* brought it to a head," Mrs. Ebert said, "but I think it started out that he was too much in favor of the Negroes, and his sermons were too full of it. And you see he's modern and his sermons are modern. He didn't quote from the Bible but he brought the biblical meanings, made them relevant to the daily problems. And the fundamentalists, they didn't like that, they wanted to hear it right from the Bible. And they wanted to hear about how we are God's chosen people and we are storing up treasures in heaven and to heck with the poor people. I mean, that's the sort of thing they wanted to hear. They wanted a tranquilizer and they wanted to be assured that everything was all right. When a minister comes in and sets you back on your feet you don't like that, it takes away your security. And they didn't like that, they didn't like somebody upsetting the apple cart.

"And then, oh, he'd had a series of seminars here in Watertown of local adults that came and listened to people from Milwaukee, Negro people, that were unhappy about their housing and were feeling oppressed. Evidently at one of those meetings, one of them, one of the over-enthusiastic Negroes, she was a secretary to Father Groppi, got a little excited and, one woman was at that, she was telling about it at this meeting.

"She said, 'Frank van der Hoogt or somebody said, "I have nothing against the Negroes, but," he says, "some of them are shiftless and some of them are oppressed and aren't neat and clean and they bring all kinds of diseases and things with them." And he said, "I don't want a lot of riots and a lot of trouble here in Watertown. We have a nice clean free town; I'd like to keep it that way for my children to grow up in."'

"'And then this Negro secretary says, "How many Negroes live here in Watertown?" and he said, "One family." And she derisively said, "One Negro family? How could we have a riot in Watertown?"'

"So this woman interpreted that as meaning they intended to have a riot in Watertown. I said to her, 'Why she just meant why are you afraid of a riot when you've only got one family here?'

"And this woman says, 'No, that isn't what she meant. What she meant was, they didn't know how they were going to pull one off.' Well, that didn't make much sense to me. But she said, 'We didn't like that seminar that you organized, and we were at that dinner and we heard those people from Father Groppi and we didn't like what they said.' And oh, then the secretary said to Frank van der Hoogt, 'You are a bigot.' And she [the woman recounting the incident] said, 'And we don't like that, our people being called bigots.'

"And so then Kromholz says, 'Well this was just a seminar. It was a series of programs for the adults.' They had all different slants on the housing situation and this happened to be one of the slants, this secretary. So then every once in awhile up would get this hysterical man and say, '*We should have this minister run out of town. Right now, right this minute.*'

"And then we stopped and the moderator said, 'Will the secretary please bring forth the minutes so we can put them in the record box?' And this young girl in the back of the room says, 'Oh, oh, I haven't got any minutes. I didn't write any. I didn't think you wanted them. The way the conversation was going I didn't think you needed them.'

"And the minister's face went way down to the floor and he said, 'You didn't *write* them? You haven't *got* any?'

"And she said, 'No, I haven't,' giggled, and to myself I blew right through the top and it was all I could do to keep from going back there and giving her a sound spanking! It was so unjust, unjust to not have records of things, especially to a person that is a journalist. I don't know why she volunteered. I suppose she was full of her awards that she'd gotten. Thought she could do a beautiful shorthand job, I don't know. But anyway she didn't write it. Maybe the whole meeting had simply overwhelmed her.

"I went up to him afterwards and I said, 'Al, I want to tell you that although I'm here in the audience, please don't count me as a dissenter. All I'm here for is I'm an inquiring reporter and I just wanted to know what the score was, since I'm supposed to be writing a monthly newsletter.'

"And he said, 'That's all right. Will you write your article?' And then right away he says, 'No, I wouldn't ask you to do that.'

"And I said, 'Well I wouldn't know what to write but I just want to tell you that I'm not one of this group in this matter.

"So then we all dispersed and you see I had come with the Bentzins so I went home with the Bentzins. And Joy said, 'I guess we told him, didn't we?'

"And I said, 'What do you mean?'

"And she says, 'Well did you notice? He didn't answer any of our questions aright out straight.'

"And I thought, what do you mean? To me he answered them. Pretty darn straight when he said, 'I haven't seen his card.' That was pretty good." Betty Ebert laughed. "But I didn't say anything 'cause I was still in this mulling stage.

"Then I came home and I got to thinking about my relationship with him. And one, I had been bereaved, my brother had died, and although he was not the minister, he *did* help me, when he heard about it. I sent the flowers over to the church and he said, 'Is there anything I can do to help you? Any advice I can give you? Just let me know.' So he *did* help me when I was bereaved.

"I was sick. I was on tranquilizers and everything else and he helped me there. And oh, I had my mother here, my dad had died and I had taken on my mother and she wanted to go to Fairhaven, that's the church's retirement home. And she'd been on the waiting list an awful long time, she was very anxious to get there, that's why I was sick, I was on tranquilizers and all that trying to take care of her and have the responsibility of it all. It was too much because she really needed professional care. So I called Al Kromholz and I said, 'Al, is there anything at all we can do to get my mother into Fairhaven sooner?' And he managed and we got her in there. So he was a great help that way.

"And I thought, well, I don't know who all these people are that say he doesn't pay attention to them. He certainly pays attention to me, and my kids. He knew them and they liked him. Mom was crazy about him.

"Then when I got home I thought, gee, I shouldn't have let this happen. I was so *mad* at myself for sitting on my hands all that night and not saying one damn thing. I mean, I should have spoken up. And all I did was sit there. The only thing I did was to go up and tell him I wasn't a dissenter, but that wasn't much and I didn't do it in front of a lot of people, I just did it privately. And I didn't tell off anybody. That's what I should have done. All I did was sit on my hands."

Mike Bentzin remembered the meeting. "And then there was this meeting. And he was going to explain himself at it. 'Course I got mixed in 'cause I was the only one with nerve to talk. If you have a guy like Kromholz, you need a guy like me. So they said find out what you can about him, Mike, and come prepared. So I got myself information on this guy and wrote it all out on cards. Oh, it had things like *Soul* and the kids in the church, and the stuff he was doing in Milwaukee, and the marching, and he wanted us to hire another minister to take care of us and that he was going to minister to the young. And that he was down South and that he got his teeth knocked out. You know about that, don't you? This's when Mann spoke at that dinner and Kromholz says, 'I have examples of police brutality, when I was down South I got beat up and there was a police car two blocks down and they didn't help me.'

"Today you don't have to be a card-carrying Communist to be a Communist," Mike Bentzin said. "But he went along with it all. He had a meeting at his house and we checked the people there and they were up from Michigan and what all. They weren't Watertown people at all except for maybe two of them.

"So at this meeting he has a tape recorder. Bill Guyer was moderator at the time and he got sucked into saying, 'This is what we're going to discuss — ' and it was just what Kromholz wanted to discuss. So somebody made a motion and it was approved unanimously that we will discuss what we want to discuss with no limitations. Because otherwise we'd talk about what *he* wanted to, and not us. Then I saw this tape recorder. 'That tape recorder is out. I know you want to tape this and then take it out of context,' I said. Well, he had the *nerve* to leave it running. It was off but it was near his hand and he could turn it off and on without being seen. Then I said, 'Pull the plug,' and he didn't, but then he saw I meant it and pulled it. The *nerve* of the guy. So I asked him some questions and he said his time was his own after Sunday and he didn't have to go visit anybody.

"So anyway I had all this information at the meeting and they said to me, 'Where'd you get it?'

"'Look,' I said, 'my information is reliable.' That meeting was the beginning of the end."

I said, I understand that this man was pretty dangerous. Did you have the F.B.I. check on him?

"Oh sure," Bentzin said. "The Chief did. And there was nothing definite on him. His father was a labor leader, apparently on the radical side. It all turned out all right."

Alan Kromholz also remembered the meeting. He said, "Well, I have some very vivid memories of that meeting. One is that — I had a very serious intent of thinking that one could dialogue with the congregation at that meeting. That turned out to be false because I believe their intent was already predetermined and that the intent was to — well, rid the church of its minister. In other words, fire him or lay the groundwork for the firing. I think they thought that might be an easy task, and within the context of the group, or the mob that was there that evening, they had a lot of support. I mean they were very secure in their position.

"The second vivid recollection of that meeting was that I had asked that the proceedings be tape recorded. It was Mr. Bentzin, the mayor of the community, who became enraged at that and said it was a Communist tactic. He would not have a tape recording of the meeting and many others agreed with him. And so, still being naively the pastor, I didn't have a tape recorded record of that meeting. I wish I did because it was in that meeting I was called a Communist by more than one individual there. The Mayor himself intimated as much.

"The third recollection is that the Mayor pointed out two things. Bentzin made the statement that I was really fomenting revolution in the entire area, that I had been in Fort Atkinson, in the home of the Reverend John Sunburn, and that I was therefore spreading my propaganda and my agitation, because shortly after my meeting with John Sunburn in his house there was a movement for open housing in Fort Atkinson. I was amazed that the

Mayor knew my activities that closely. But it is true that I had dinner with Sunburn on the night, et cetera, that the Mayor had outlined. It was part of a ministerial association gathering that we had at his home.

"The second thing then that the Mayor said that evening that surprised me and disturbed me and that today yet makes me quite angry — he went on to point out that I had been away from my parish, that I had been in Iowa. As I recall it and as my family recalls it, because I came home quite shook that evening, he pointed out that I had been in Cedar Falls, Waterloo, Iowa."

Kromholz told me that he and his family went to Iowa about a week or so prior to the meeting because of the abuse the family had been getting.

"And the Mayor was very quick," he went on, "to point out that not only was I agitating in the Watertown community and spreading that agitation to the Fort Atkinson community, but that I was carrying it *out* into the Midwest. He seemed to know my every move. There was only one person that knew where I was going [his general destination, not his route]. That was the Chief of Police, Mr. Mann. So I have every, well, I believe that the Mayor therefore had surveillance which simply makes me believe yet today that the leadership of Watertown was very fascist, gestapo, and I think the meeting was a very difficult and frustrating meeting because there was no record, because no matter how I tried to dialogue, charges were simply laid out in an angry and violent manner by the people there. What is most frustrating about the meeting was, at least to me, the fact of the gestapo activities of the Mayor."

I asked Chief Mann about surveillance. I said that because the Mayor had confronted Kromholz with every place that he had been in Iowa he felt that he must have been followed. He didn't see any other way that the Mayor could have known.

Mann said, "No, he definitely was not followed. I'm sure that Reverend Kromholz told somebody else that he was leaving. Matter of fact, he never even told me where he was going. He called me and told me and asked if we would watch the house because he had received threats and so on and so forth. And again, when people get involved in I don't care what it is, but when somebody starts making statements publicly, naturally, there's going to be opposition. There's going to be people who think just the opposite of what I think. But believe me, I did not mention one word that Kromholz was leaving and — I've heard this too, that I'd called the F.B.I., God, I had everybody in the country following him, and this information did not go any farther than myself. Now I'm sure that somebody else in town knew where he was going. I think he told me that he was going down to visit his brother or something and I didn't even know where his brother lived. And I'm trying to think. I think we even had the name of somebody that had the key to the house. If there was a fire or something and we had to get in there. Or there would be some reason why we had to check the house or something. But we definitely did not follow him. I mean, in the first place the F.B.I. wouldn't follow this guy, *nobody* would follow him, I mean he wasn't that big a man. There's no reason for following him. I mean, he'd done nothing. I could care less where he or anybody else goes. But *I* did not tell the Mayor. I did not tell anybody. Just kept it to myself.

"We certainly didn't have anybody following him. The one thing that we did do, I did have the squad taking down license numbers when I knew that there was going to be a meeting over at his house, and the reason for that is that I want to know who's in this town. I do want to know who's in this town. Whether they are going to be troublemakers, and if so, I want to be tipped off ahead of time. And again, this is our job."

And there were troublemakers?

"There were people there that were known to be agitators."

Again I asked Al Kromholz about going out of town.

Didn't the Frieses know where you were going?

"No," Kromholz said, "*No* one knew."

Who'd you leave your key with?

"No one."

Had you told the Chief of Police exactly what your route was or where you were going?

"Not at all. I told him we were going to Iowa. I *might* have told him we were going to Cedar Falls but I don't recall that. I don't believe I did."

But the Mayor knew you were in Cedar Falls?

"Yes. Which makes me draw the conclusion I was followed."

You're not saying that Chief Mann necessarily did it?

"No," Kromholz said. "I'm saying that the Mayor — now, who the Mayor used or what was done, I don't know."

I asked Kromholz if he had made any agreement to compromise at that meeting.

He paused. "Well, I don't know — it's a long time now. Yeah, I think in a sense we made a compromise that *yes* we'll both attempt to work together. That I as Pastor would go back and attempt to take a biblical thrust at the gospel text on Sunday."

And did you in fact do that?

"Oh yes, I think so," he said. "Which led me only to a deeper commitment to attempt to make the gospel word meaningful within the context of the times that we were engaged in. I had never read the Gospel with, with such — you know words almost, not almost, they did, they just — came alive and they blew up as you read the Gospel preparing for Sunday morning. You said, *God* this is our situation, this related to — to what the Diaconate in the church wouldn't do or to what the City Council won't do within the context of the city. I mean this is why I said at the time, and I say again that basically, and I don't just say this about the Watertown congregation but I think about most Christian congregations, that they are theologically ignorant — and illiterate. Because they believe to biblically base sermons is to talk about the Good Samaritan and what a *wonderful* guy this was, better than the Jew who walked by, and the priest, or Levite who walked by [Luke 10:29–37]. Kinds of things that Christians like to take little pot shots at Jews, for not being turned on to the needs of the world. The priest who they somehow conjure up in their minds, the Catholic priest. But the Good Samaritan, who is a good Protestant, he washed the guy up, cleans him up, says here, take my money. And they like the little stories but they don't really understand what is involved in that parable, why it was used, what application it has to today's life. Or they don't make any application to today's life. We just tell stories about how long the Emmaus Road is [Luke 24:13–35]. It runs from Jericho to Jerusalem and men spend great thirty minutes of sermonic time talking about that glorious road and how long it is. And say if you just walk that road, if you trudge it through every day, someday you're going to get from Jericho to Jerusalem and you're going to be resurrected, saved. That's a biblical sermon. But if you tear it apart, I think it's revolutionary."

How?

"It's talking about change. Change in action, attitude, belief, and saying — what is it saying? Saying get involved with your brother. If he's bleeding stop and get off and make damn sure you put him on your donkey. Don't just look at him. *Take* him along with you. *Spend* your money, get your clothes dirty. Find a way to heal him. Change society. Everybody get off their donkey. Get off your ass. That would have been a good sermon if I had thought of the title, 'Get Off Your Ass, Baby.' "

11

During this time the Kromholzes had been receiving harassing phone calls. I asked him about them, when they started.

"That was a very painful experience. When did they start? I'm not sure. I think around October, that fall."

Had he had threatening phone calls before the November meeting?

"Yes," Kromholz said, "Harassing phone calls. I'm not sure they were threatening at that point."

I asked how often he got them.

"It's hard to say. Twice a week, three times a week."

I asked what the pattern was, if they continued steadily.

"Very interesting, as I recall it. I had gone to the phone company and the police and asked for a surveillance on my line. Because they had gotten somewhat frequent, and threatening."

When did they get threatening?

"I think around November. Ruth got most of the calls. She was home, I wasn't home."

(Although I would have liked to, I did not speak to Ruth Kromholz about the conflict in Watertown. The experience had been an extremely painful one for her and she did not want to discuss it with me two years after the fact.)

Kromholz continued, "Although it seemed like occasionally, it seemed like I'd walk in the door and just get set down, and a phone call would come. And at times nothing was said. Just a call, a dead line, and then somebody would hang up. Sometimes there were funny ones and where people would call and say, 'You're the devil.' "

Did he think it was more than one person? There were different voices?

"Oh yeah. I think so. 'You're the devil. You're going to burn in hell. You're to be out saving souls, not creating — you know. I'll pray for you, brother.' And so I would always say, 'Well, pray for me because apparently I need it.' And, either way, I needed it. Let me come back. What was most interesting to me is that when I asked in the fall or somewhere in there for the surveillance on my phone, the calls basically stopped. It was *very* very funny. At least Ruth and I thought it was funny."

What do you mean by funny? I asked.

"As if someone in the telephone company knew that the line was under surveillance and the word got passed. Then I had it removed. I mean nothing was coming, so I mentioned it to the phone company, 'Well, nothing's coming.' Then the calls did occur again. I don't recall if immediately after, or whenever. But I was upset enough to believe, and I'm sure that this was just my feeling, that *some*how the phone company, or the people involved in the phone company, I think you might understand this, Mr. Bertling was one of my adversaries, he worked for the phone company. It became quite difficult to trust anyone. I simply thought it was useless to go and have a tap put on my line, surveillance, and so we'd simply receive the calls and listen. And I wasn't too threatened by them."

Did you put the tracer on again?

"No, no. For a long period of time we did not. Then again in the spring, when they got violent, we asked for it on again." He told me the tenor of several were "'You goddamn nigger lover. We're going to get you.' 'Well, what do you mean by getting me, mister?' 'We're gonna push your nose through the other side of your head.' That was the most violent and threatening one I think I got."

Mayor Bentzin said, "And he said he was getting threatening phone calls. So we put this thing on to check phone calls and Mann told him we'd give him surveillance. And do you know, not *one* call came through. Not even one. And so we told him that and then he gave up on that. He was always looking for publicity."

I asked Bentzin, Do you think he got any threatening phone calls?

"No, of course he didn't get any."

Chief Mann said, "Threats on Kromholz? I don't believe it."

In the midst of the highly charged opposition to Alan Kromholz, a community group to promote equal rights in Watertown was born. The Watertown Human Relations Council focused its attention on open housing and then on migrant workers. They also wrote a letter to Chief Mann inquiring why riot equipment had been bought. Not surprisingly, Al Kromholz was instrumental in the Council's formation and was its first vice chairman.

Enthusiasm for the Human Relations Council was very high. Kathy Isaacson, president of the League of Women Voters, wrote the following in her journal and in a letter:

"November 14th. A historic day in the city of Watertown. . . . There was a public meeting at St. Bernard's for Dr. Victor Hoffman to talk about fair housing — the ethics of power. It was a fine talk and lots of questions were asked which led to, of course, what can we do? Close to two hundred people were there too, and it was P.T.A. night. Anyway, there was a motion to form a steering committee for a Watertown Council on Human Relations and eight people were nominated."

IV

There was another approach to resolving the conflict in the church besides that manifested in the November 17 meeting. According to the moderator, Bill Guyer, three men had met with the association minister before the meeting in November. He recalled that Weir McQuoid, Palmer Freres, who is the church treasurer, and he, Guyer, met with Roy Albersworth one evening for several hours and that Albersworth "suggested that we get a group of people together that represented all factions in the church and discuss this whole thing and try to come to some consensus and talk to Al Kromholz." Guyer remembered that they did this, had several meetings, and spent a lot of time on it. The result of the meetings was a letter to Al Kromholz dated December 2, 1967. It began:

Dear Alan:

On November 29th, a group of concerned members of our congregation met to consider the problems that are facing our church. In the fact of many members wanting to withdraw financial support, it was felt that an attempt must be made to clarify matters and to prevent further deterioration. This group represented a good cross-section of our membership and the discussion brought out varied points of view. While we did not have complete agreement, the results of the discussion are presented here as recommendations to you for policy and action, that if pursued, could possibly lead to healing of the wounds that are now present. They are presented hopefully and prayerfully as a means of saving this church which is dear to us as well as to many others whom we attempted to represent.

We do not feel that we are trying to, nor should we, deny you your convictions. As our spiritual leader, we desire that, through the word of God, you present your convictions to us; but that you recognize our right and desire to solve problems in a manner that does not violate our own personal convictions. We also feel the individual problems of a congregation are many and varied and the repetition of any one subject will tend to drive members to attempt to find the answers they are seeking in some other place.

The letter went on to ask "that political issues be avoided and that controversial social issues be offered in a spirit of fair play." It mentioned that there was a feeling in the congregation that Kromholz's social action concerns had taken much time and energy away from his duties as minister. It said that the comment was made that it was the means and not the end that caused disagreement. It mentioned *Soul*:

The publication of *Soul* has caused a great deal of trouble. You have been accused of teaching our people the thoughts that were expressed and while this is debatable, the paper certainly caused embarrassment to our members. In connection with this, the use of church equipment and facilities without supervision has been questioned.

The last paragraph began:

Alan, we as a representative group of this congregation, appeal to you to accept this letter in the spirit in which it is offered. We approach you with an appeal to lead our group back together again and to replace anger and frustration with respect and love.

Bill Guyer and I discussed the letter. Guyer, a soft-spoken man in his fifties, said, "I felt if anything was going to be done to save the situation at all, the cards really had to be laid on the table and this is what it was and so I didn't try and pull any punches. This is the way I felt the majority of the people felt. Well, it seemed to me that Al appeared to be willing to give this a chance, to *try* to meet people half way. I must say that looking back on it now, I think it was too late. I don't think anything that he could have done really would have saved the situation because I think there was people that, it's a strange thing but you can see hate in the church, and it was there. They were just —"

I interrupted, But at the time you didn't think that?

Guyer replied, "No, I thought possibly — Mayor Bentzin remarked to me one day I'm too naive. And maybe he's right. Some of these people that I've known for a long long time and I've liked, disappointed me in that I didn't really think that they would really make any attempt. I don't think that if he had turned from black to white they would have accepted him. I just kind of have that feeling that it had gotten to the point where they wanted no part of him, they'd just as much as say they hated him. They hated his guts, they wanted him out of there, if he wouldn't leave, they were gonna leave. That's all there was to it."

I asked if he was alarmed at the sick calls Kromholz was neglecting.

"Well, I think this is something that was over-emphasized. He made calls, perhaps he didn't do as many as he could — I think the critical calls, the sick people, I don't think he neglected this so terribly. But I don't think

I've ever known a minister that satisfied everybody as far as calls. So I didn't put as much on this as quite a few people did."

Discussing Kromholz's sermons, Guyer said, "They were presented in a manner that said in effect this situation exists and *this* is what should be done about it. And I think this is what antagonized a great many people. He said, 'This situation exists, here is a great man who is trying to do something about it,' Father Groppi, '*I* am going to help him, and *you* must too.' And they wouldn't take this, you see. I think many of them thought if he on his own had gone and done whatever he wanted to, they still would have accepted, although there would have been criticism. But they would not accept him saying *you* must do this, or you must believe this, and you must believe that he is right. They didn't believe this, they *still* don't believe it to this day. There's a tremendous problem here. He came into a church here that had, the backbone of this church has belonged to this church for a *long,* long, long time. A lot of them were raised in this church and lived all their life here."

I asked him how his concept of the ministry differs from Al Kromholz's.

"Well, I suppose it's a very basic thing. It's something that certainly is being argued all over the place. But it would seem to me that if a man accepts a call and comes to a church, it seems to me that he *has* to come and minister to those people — which you see is where the thing went haywire. Because Al wasn't doing this. Ministering to some people but only to those who felt the same way he did. And I realize this is a very controversial thing these days. This is happening all over that ministers are saying the church is not good this way. The church has to step out and change and get into it, get with it, as they say. But this is where the real problem comes in, the very very difficult thing because these people, these older people, there's *no* way that they can possibly do what these younger people — they *can't* approve this, it's right inside of them, they feel this shouldn't be in the church, and it just tears them apart. And they're not going to take it."

Guyer, who considered himself a middle-of-the-roader in the church conflict, along with his close friends, the van der Hoogts, is not extreme in his political views either. I asked how he would describe America today.

He said, "Seems to me it's a country with some — in the midst of great change, with a lot of people doing a great deal of very deep thinking, trying to figure out just what *is* happening, and what should happen and what direction it should go." Guyer spoke slowly and deliberately, thinking out what he meant as he was saying it.

"Certainly a lot of changes are going to take place. I think there's a lot of dangerous things happening but I have a strong feeling it's all going to work out for the best sooner or later. I think some very stern measures are going to have to be taken though. I think there's things that have gone to the point where it's getting close to a breakdown and these will *have* to be controlled. But I think even our present administration, and many people think that they are insensitive, I don't feel they are, it's certainly a conservative philosophy that's in control but I think that they realize that changes have to be made too, and that changes *are* being made."

I asked what he thought of the war on poverty, paused, and said, I don't know if it's still on, but as it started out to be?

"Well you get into these arguments about what should be done," Guyer said. "I think I do favor what the Administration's trying to do now. We have to face this. People object greatly to the bad things that happen in welfare. I think that most people feel compassion, they would like to help people, but it *really* draws their ire to see people getting fat on these things and it also draws their ire to see people that won't try to help themselves. I think this is kinda tied in with the program the Administration's trying to promote with the guaranteed income, to fix it so that there is an incentive for people to work and yet to keep people from starving. I think we've all, most people do feel they are their brother's keepers for those people that need help, but *gee*, it makes them mad to see somebody refuse to help themselves."

Do you think that if a man wants to make a decent living in this country today he can? That the opportunity is there?

"Well, certainly not in all cases. Without any training you can't. Things have become more and more technical and right now it's hard but there has been a situation for many years where anybody that was willing could get some work. But they might only make fifty dollars a week, and how can you live on only fifty dollars a week?"

What do you think of defense spending?

"Well," Guyer said, "I just — you hate to see this money go this way but the way the world is there's just no question about what we have to do. We've been placed in a position where we represent one side in the world. There's two sides. And if we don't do it, I can't believe that the other side is just going to say, 'Well fine, you're not doing this so we won't.' I don't believe that's the situation. Hopefully that will be the situation some day but I don't think it's here yet."

I told Bill Guyer that Mayor Bentzin said he thought the Communist Party had a lot to do with what was happening in the country. I asked him what he thought.

"Well, that's where we — we don't agree. He was the one who called me naive and it was because I didn't agree with him that some people were Communist."

In this town?

"Yeah. I don't think — for instance he was sure that Al Kromholz was Communist. This goes back and I think a lot of young people can't quite realize the stigma of being a Communist."

We didn't live through McCarthy, I said.

"And back before that. This was about the worst thing you could possibly be was a Communist. But this has calmed down through the years now and there's Communists in this country, they're not crucified anymore. They're accepted and they openly say that they're Communists. And by law, they have every right to be a Communist if they want to be."

I asked Guyer what he thought of the war in Vietnam.

"Well, I think that's something that everybody would like to — sweep under the rug. I think it's been oversimplified. I don't agree with the people that say we should just up and walk out. I just don't see how we can possibly do that. I think it's unfortunate that we ever got involved.

"Well, look, let me put it this way, after World War II ended we were left as the *only* country that really had the resources and was capable of doing anything to prevent a tremendous Communist expansion. We filled a vacuum in Europe, we filled a vacuum in Japan, to some extent in the Southeast. We by ourselves put the world back on its feet, there's no question, and that includes Russia too. So, if we hadn't done this, what would be the situation? I think we accepted certain facts, we accepted we couldn't exist in wealth while the great majority of the world groveled in misery and we started to do things about this.

"It isn't just a real simple thing. I think many young people say that it's wrong to kill. And it is, *but* if somebody is trying to kill you, you're gonna defend yourself.

"I think this is where the militants are missing the boat too. If they go too far — "

Frank Isaacson, husband of the president of the League of Women Voters, was on the committee that drafted the December 2 letter to Kromholz. Isaacson said, "I went to see Bill about this letter, privately. And to try and get him to tone it down. And he did, some. It says here, 'We desire that through the word of God you present your convictions.' It seems to me that's backwards. Present the word of God through your convictions is the way it should be. I mean maybe that's a minor point but it seems to me that's representative of the question. And see, that demonstrates the lack of understanding between them and us, and them and me. Because once you get by that, then you got a whole other bag of tricks. It should be that the word of God is not the means for you to convince us, but your convictions are the means for you to present the word of God to us. Once you get that, then you have to accept a whole bunch of things that the word of God means. I asked Bill to just change that, to just reverse it, but he wouldn't do it. He said, 'Well, it doesn't really make any difference, does it?' What we're really interested in is the presentation and the just way to behave and all that crap. I thought I had him convinced and he said he'd do it but then it came out the other way."

Was the committee hostile?

"Well certain members — terrible." Isaacson laughed. "I guess I'd have to consider myself the furthest left of this group. And I had some allies. Like Harry Miller was very close and I'd say that Mrs. Jim Jaye was understanding. And Jerry Mallach was understanding. Clark Derleth was openly hostile. I think Ben Thauer and Gordon Frater are very similar and I *think* they like me." He laughed. "I mean I just feel — and I like them — and I feel that maybe they'd like not to hurt me. So they didn't say anything that was — but Clark Derleth would have no truck with that. He didn't mind hurting. But some of them would say I just don't see why it's necessary. Ben Thauer. Gordon Frater would tell the story about the businessmen, how in business we respect people who are aggressive but we don't want aggressiveness in our ministry. Yeomans was talking about saving the church."

Frank Isaacson is in his middle thirties, a tall sophisticated looking man who told me he is shy. "Others think it arrogance," he said. He is an architect and is not happy with the present state of architecture, nor with a lot of other things. "I could just walk out — anytime — and not come back. Until I did. There's something called the executive slump. It happens to about thirty-five-year-old executives. They're very successful and then they suddenly slump and fail. He has his suburban house, is supporting his three cars, two boats and a horse, has his country club dues and payments to make and his family to support and then he says, 'So what? I don't want this,' and he starts failing."

Isaacson, who does not have a suburban house, three cars, two boats or a horse, and only contemplates executive slump, discussed the present state of architecture with me. "What most people overlook is what's there. And more and more what I look for is the uniqueness of a site or a set of conditions. Because for too long they more or less ignored it and said that our building will be so beautiful, so fine, that whatever ills there were existing, it would all come out okay, on the basis of our *great* design. Now that happens to be a bunch of crap, I believe."

Why?

"Our building isn't that important. Any given building is simply not that important. What is there, all around the building, the *reality* that exists in any set of conditions is more important than what you put on it, I believe. Probably there are exceptions but the average building that the average architect does kind of ignores all that and concentrates his effort rather on how good his part will be and not worry about what's wrong with it. We've been trained, in terms of our own ego, to behave in a certain way. We think we can solve the existing problems by our *clever* design. Sometimes we know the part that's the problem is outside of our control and so we don't even recognize that. That's not even reality. We think in terms of well, then we'll just have to make it all the more beautiful, to compensate for that. I think it's the loser."

After concern with the site, what else is important?

"Well, I mean *all* the conditions that are there," Frank Isaacson said. "I don't mean just the ground, the earth. I mean everything else, the people, the cars, everything, all of the parts that are there. After that, that's all there is. You can be very clever about your own building. A given building can be *really* nice but in terms of the cityscape it don't make a damn unless — I mean it may or may not depending on how it responds to the rest that's there. So I guess I'm kind of coming to realize that the larger planning, or the recognition, it's not really planning, it's just recognition and acknowledgment of what's there."

I asked him how he would describe America today.

"Well, I'm afraid it doesn't work very well. I don't think it is as responsive to change as it's supposed to be. As they would, *they,* I mean the Agnews would have you believe. Reagan said something this morning that to me is really pretty true and a real problem, in his interview on the TV, the Today Show. He said that there exists a bureaucratic problem where a lot of things he wanted to get done, even though I don't agree with probably what they were, he said that there exists a bureaucracy that is almost impossible to move. And that might be a problem that is even bigger than the Agnews and Reagans. These people, the professional bureaucrat, looks upon the elected official as sort of a temporary nuisance. And maybe that's a bigger problem. Just absolutely overwhelming. It seems like once it's started there's no way to stop it. The same thing in our business. We try to get committees to work and put more people on more committees to make unworkable ones work and it just doesn't work."

How else would you describe it?

Very emphatically Isaacson said, "Sad." He laughed. "I don't know, it's not a very nice place to be. But I don't know what to do about it. It's pretty depressing I think for the person, quote liberal unquote, kind of thirty-five-year-old professional because you're really coming into a supposedly productive time of your life, and you feel maybe you are personally, but socially it's," the next two words were drawn out, "so — bad. Depressing."

Discussing the lack of community of modern man Isaacson said, "I think if you could sort of sum it up, which is dangerous, but socially man has not come along as far as he has technically. And maybe the nature of man just doesn't adapt as well to social change. Just takes longer. And the technology is outside of man and the social part is not. I'm sure that's what it is. That's the basic problem. It shows up in this rootlessness. I think they are a lot more rootless. I think it's too bad. Obviously I'm rootless. I've moved around a lot and this is the way it works. And I consider moves again. I don't know if it's part of the economic system or not. I'm sure it's all interwoven. I'm not sure if being in one spot is a prerequisite for a sense of community.

"Frankly, I feel alienated from this community. I think rootlessness is here to stay. Maybe even searching for roots is outmoded. Growing up in one place is outmoded. Since that's what your adult life is about, maybe it's better to have learned it young? Even parenthood as we know it may be outmoded. Probably is. Why take a chance? Use someone else's tested, tried, and true sperm."

You've got to be kidding, I said. You don't really believe it?

"Oh yeah," Frank Isaacson said, "I think I do believe it. I think it's just my own hangup that equates my manhood with my sperm. And I do. But that's going to be outmoded too."

v

Frank Isaacson was assistant moderator of the church and remembered chairing the December Church Council meeting when endorsement of open housing was brought up again after having been tabled in November.

"Well, I think that's the first meeting I ever chaired," he said. "As such, for this kind of a thing. And it was much different from a club meeting or anything like that." He recalled that Bill Guyer had called him about six o'clock in the evening and told him he was sick. "I didn't even realize that I was vice moderator. I don't know if Guyer was really sick or trying to get off the hook.

"We took care of routine business and then we had to talk about open housing. And Myrl Pauli moved that we adopt the resolution, in support of open housing. Addressed to the City Council in support of open housing. I believe there was a second though I don't remember who." Isaacson told me he was very naive then and didn't do any preparation for the meeting. He remembered that certain board members said they couldn't vote on it because their board had not reached a consensus and they therefore could not represent their board.

"Well, then they also said it's improper for a few people to say that the First Congregational Church is in favor of it. I said, 'Well, that's fine, I agree with that, but it doesn't say that the Church Council can't say it, that we as the Council — we're not speaking for the church, we're speaking for the Council and all the members of the Council.' But they said they still felt it was unfair, that the only way it could be fair was if the Congregational Church was to be involved, the Congregational Church would have to make the decision and that's the way the Congregational Church did their business. Take it to a Congregational meeting.

"Anyway, that kind of went around like that. In fact, I don't even believe it got a second. I think I violated procedure in asking them to discuss it, hoping that I could get a second. But I know that Myrl withdrew the motion and she was in tears and she was really upset about it. She said, 'Well, I guess I'll have to withdraw the motion.' I couldn't second it."

It was decided that the open housing issue would be decided and voted on by the congregation at the annual meeting in January.

Open Housing II

The same night that the Church Council met, December 5, the Watertown City Council took its last vote on open housing. An open housing ordinance had been presented the week before by Chuck Yeomans, the chairman of the welfare committee, the committee to which the issue had originally been referred October 16. It had met with stiff opposition the previous week and was laid over. After the Monday night committee of the whole meeting on December 4, the *Daily Times* said,

> Chances of adopting a fair housing law in Watertown appear slim, based on comments made by aldermen at their committee of the whole meeting last night.
>
> All councilmen who made comments, except one, indicated that they were not in favor of adopting a fair housing ordinance in Watertown.

The *Times* went on to say,

> There was no prejudice on the part of the councilmen who expressed the feeling that there is not a need for an ordinance of this kind in Watertown. The feeling prevailed to wait until such a need developed. . . .

Alderman Nuernberg declared that "anyone can buy land here. No one is refused if he wants to buy or rent a home." He added that "there's no lack of equal opportunity here." He also said "that our city is open to everybody. We all have been created alike. That's the way it's been and that's the way it will stay."

Alderman Gerloff observed "that we never have run into this problem."

Alderman Ruesch commented that a proposed fair housing law "has been kicked all out of proportion." He stated that "If I would find discrimination here, I'd be the first to sponsor an ordinance. But no one has been discriminated against here. We have no problems here.". . . .

Alderman Schwenker reported that he recently visited with a good friend who is a Negro. He said that his friend told him that if he were a member of the City Council of Watertown he'd vote against the proposed ordinance. . . .

On December 5, open housing in Watertown was tabled for the last time. According to the official minute book, "Alderman Fredrich moved the ordinance be tabled until such time as Watertown needs an ordinance of this type." The vote was seven to seven and the Mayor cast the deciding ballot to table.

Public Opinion: Open Housing
"Naturally we're going to have more problems among them than we do among the whites, not because God made them inferior but because we held them down over this period of years. But we've *got* to keep the Groppis from dominating them. We don't want them to get a situation where they have more respect for an outlaw Mafia than they do for their own government. That's what we've got to stop. And we stopped it. I think we did a good job here in Watertown. There was a tie vote and the Mayor cast the deciding ballot to vote down this ordinance, and we stopped it."

Bernard Traeger

"Well, that I think would have passed without much furore if it hadn't been for the way he [Kromholz] went about it. Oh, he went up to the City Council, hollered around, made a big show and created a lot of ill will. Well, yes, I agree that there should be an open housing ordinance. But as I say, I think that would have passed with no trouble if he hadn't made such a racket."

Peg Buckland

"I think it's *ridiculous* what happened, I mean it's ridiculous that it wasn't passed. I honestly think that the reason it wasn't passed was because it was blown up, it was out in the open."

Barb van der Hoogt

In a letter:
    "There were a few days when I seriously wanted to suggest to the Chamber of Commerce that they change that sign at the entrance to the city to read, 'If you think the way we do (or if you're willing to keep your mouth shut), Welcome to Watertown.' The fair housing ordinance has been tabled because we don't have any prejudice here. What a lousy thing to do."

Kathy Isaacson

Mike Bentzin described the whole dynamic of the open housing battle in Watertown. "See, Fries slipped in an open housing ordinance in the envelope with the agenda but it has to come through an alderman or mayor. We weren't having problems. This Human Relations Council was making the problem. Well, finally some alderman introduced the ordinance and we kept laying it over and laying it over and finally they said, 'Let's vote on it.' This one night this civil rights group loaded the gallery with people. This was on a Tuesday. The night before when we'd had a conference it looked like nobody wanted it. On Tuesday some of them were scared politically and voted seven to seven on a motion to lay it over. So then I had to break the tie and they were all smiling. I think maybe they'd planned it out before so I would have to be on the hook. So I voted to lay it over. I didn't vote against it, but to lay it over. I wouldn't veto them but I wouldn't get involved in that so I just voted to lay over, not *against* it. Anyone could bring it up any time they want. They still could."

I asked why people wanted the bill and Bentzin said, "Just because it was popular."

At that point Mrs. Bentzin interjected, "So what's this Human Relations Council needed for? We've been helping the migrants for years. We go out there and teach them English and how to use a sewing machine and how to make clothes in our style. Why, just the other day we brought Mexican food to a Mexican family. And they had such a nice house. Beautiful, so neat and clean."

Chuck Yeomans was the alderman who was chairman of the welfare committee and who moved that the fair housing ordinance be adopted. I asked him why he was for the ordinance and he said, "I was for the ordinance because I don't want to keep anybody out of Watertown. We have hired Mexicans in this business [the Ira L. Henry Company] and we will continue to do so, who are not a part of the homogeneous Watertown inheritance, or nationality. And for instance, if a black person would come here with the right kind of work background, I would hire him, and I think my superintendent [Yeoman's employee] would go along with it. That's the way I feel."

I asked why people voted against the ordinance.

"Out of suspicion, I think. That it would bring somebody in Watertown that would cause trouble, in relationships. I think there still is an inherent suspicion mostly because of no contact with people of foreign color or background."

Dave Fries had told me he wondered if the vote wasn't set up to tie so the Mayor could have the glory of breaking the vote and defeating the ordinance. I asked Yeomans if the tie vote was set up for one reason or another.

He said, "I would have a comment on that. I definitely believe there was no connivance as far as getting a certain number to vote for or against. To be perfectly honest, which I can be now that I'm out of politics, without any hesitation — I was pretty honest as far as telling people what I thought on the Council — but there was no pressure, or no push on the side of open housing ordinance on the Council. I think the Council was pushed from the outside. But no individual member did any politicking for. In fact, I was very much surprised that the open housing ordinance got half the vote. I was very surprised. I didn't push it. Mainly because, and I still feel, that there hasn't been an occasion I could feel was verified that anybody was prevented from coming into Watertown. I don't have any evidence of it, and if there was, I would certainly want to push for an open housing referendum. That's the way I feel."

Just before I left, Yeomans commented, "I think this should be a wide open town. I even think there should be some Negro families here. 'Course they should live on the outskirts for awhile until people got acquainted with them."

II

Throughout the struggle for open housing there had been constant rumors related to it, and to Father Groppi. Sydney McQuoid recalled one incident. "It was a night when nothing really was going on. It was a warm night, in November, I think, and somebody had called Father Thilman and said they'd heard a rumor that school was going to be let out and they were all going to march up and down town, people were going to march, the grade schools were going to march, and Father Groppi was going to come in and they were going to bring in blacks and they were going to have a big march. I remember Father Thilman responded with this really funny comment, I don't remember exactly, but something like, 'Maybe it should be here!' Well, he told me that and that night, well, Kathy [Smith] liked to play jokes and stuff and we said [in a very W. C. Fields tone], 'Well, people believe there's going to be a march? Maybe we ought to do something about it.'

"So we were walking up and down Main, everybody just hangs around, and there just happened to be two black people that stopped at Schuett's. They were driving through town, there's a fishing area outside of town where a lot of black people go, and they just happened to stop around eight o'clock and that's just prime time. And so Kathy and I were running down Main Street and getting people off to the side and saying, 'Psss, pssss,' and people would look, and there were state troopers driving up and down Main Street, I think just one or two patrol cars. I think the police [city police] asked them to come in, and then the police were driving around just all night, all night.

"And this wasn't unusual at all. There were a lot of rumors like this. And I didn't even hear a lot of them, I'm sure. You see, I think a lot of them would start when these people would come to bridge clubs and they'd say something and then it'd be bigger and bigger and bigger, and then they'd go to another bridge club, some of these people have four bridge clubs a week."

The Isaacsons said the rumors were related to "what would happen if you have open housing and you invite, in effect, tell all those people that they should come out here."

Kathy Isaacson said, "They would come out in droves."

I asked who said that.

Frank Isaacson said, "Well see, nobody ever says it. Except that somebody says that, 'Well I heard that somebody else said,' or 'they said,' or *they* said' — "

Mrs. Isaacson said, "Or you overhear something at the meat counter or the grocery store or something. You could listen to the call-in program at the radio station. I guess that got lively sometime. There, that's anonymous people calling."

George Bausch, a congregation member, told me, "Everybody was scared at the time this marching was going on in Milwaukee. But anyway, there was rumor that perhaps people from Milwaukee might be coming out here to Watertown."

To march, to riot?

"Both, both, who knows? They were going to come out here and people were afraid of their properties."

III

I thought Walt and Virginia Goodie, Watertown's only black family, might be interesting to talk to. At first Mr. Goodie did not want to talk with me and told me he was busy and could he call me? I persisted and he finally said he thought he and his wife could give me fifteen or twenty minutes. He later told me that the real reason he let me come over was because he knew voices over the telephone and he liked mine.

The Goodies live on a commercially zoned street, between the Schmutzler Furniture Store and the First United Congregational Church of Christ. Their small living room has faded magenta wallpaper with rows of cream palm trees. The carpet carries out the motif in a faded white floral pattern. More striking are the low lighting fixture hung by a chain from the ceiling, the two television sets, the desk, the dozens of snapshots on the desk, the large couch with piles of music stacked on it, the grand piano with more music piled on the piano bench, the vibraharp, the marimba with birthday cards on it, and in a corner, a bass violin. The room smelled purple. Mr. and Mrs. Goodie had just been reading the Bible to each other and their copies were set on the covered card table between the piano and the couch. They are both over seventy-five years old.

Mr. Goodie said, "We've been here twenty-two years and there's no more prejudice against us than other people. I've never heard anyone call me anything to my face, and if they do, well, they talk about each other too, the Catholics, the Irish. No matter where you go, there's a race problem. We moved here so we could put our children through the university and we didn't know if we wanted them to go to Milwaukee or Madison."

I asked, But why Watertown?

"Well, honey," he said, "we'd been all over the country and Canada and we'd seen all kinds of things and we knew there'd be less prejudice here than in Milwaukee or Madison. Well, not prejudice because that's here as much, but discrimination. Here if someone talks up against you twenty people or more even will defend you."

I asked what they thought of the open housing ordinance they tried to pass and Mr. Goodie said, "Naturally I'm in favor of open housing but every town around here they get all upset. They get worked up, 'Are they gonna move in here?' but they shouldn't worry because until they have jobs for people why should they worry about open housing? Nobody's gonna want to move in here unless they can work. But the point is, as long as I keep my mouth shut, I know what I know, no one can condemn me for my thoughts and it's gonna stir up ill feeling. We have some friends in town we talk freely with, some wonderful friends, but to give any public talks on housing, prejudice, I don't do that. We don't have any problem ourselves, we're just happy, thank God. We like it here very much.

"When we first came to Watertown we had a hard time getting a place. This was a tea house, not a regular place, but we like it, no neighbors around too close. We came here to give a concert, sponsored by the Methodist Church. We came here Friday and spent Sunday looking over town to see if we'd like to live here. We found a place near Western Avenue over there and practically bought it. We agreed on $12,000 or $12,500, I forget which, and that night at the concert, Monday night, I announced from the stage that we were settling here and had found a place. I knew people would find out anyway so instead of sneaking I thought it was much better to just come out with it. The next morning we went over to sign the papers and finish the deal and he said the deal was off, he just couldn't sell it to me and he was acting very apologetic. I said, 'Let's be frank, some of your neighbors brought pressure, right?' And he wouldn't say anything and I kept telling him that and finally he got mad, not at me, but at the people, and he said, 'I'll tell you, nobody's gonna tell me what I can do. Give me $14,000 and I'll sell it to you.' I said no thanks, nobody was gonna take advantage of me like that.

"So at this time we traveled around and lived in a bus, and we just continued to live in the bus in Watertown for two months. Finally the woman who owned this place got mad at people that we couldn't get a house and called me up and asked me to come over, and sold it to me. We had tried about four or five houses and every one turned out the same way."

He told me that two years ago they gave him an eightieth-birthday banquet at the Methodist Church. "You just can't ask more than that." I asked him how they made their living in Watertown and Mr. Goodie said, "My wife taught piano. I taught marimbas. I'm a piano repairman. And I was a Fuller Brush man. Now I sell McNess products."

The phone rang and Mr. Goodie got up to answer it. Mrs. Goodie and I smiled at each other and I asked her what they did before they lived in Watertown.

"Well, first we were in the vaudeville," she said. "We sang and played. That's all, no dancing. And Daddy did jokes and it was *wonderful*."

She showed me a handbill:

Not Another Group like this in all America
Walt Goodie
presents his Marimba-Vibraharp Choir
in a Concert. Sacred-Classical Music
An Original Idea in Wholesome Entertainment.
This you must see to fully appreciate!

A poster on the couch said much the same thing and

billed them as "America's most Versatile Family of Negro Artists."

Mrs. Goodie said, "We were in the vaudeville thirty years. We met in, let's see, '23 I think, and that's when we started. Daddy and I get along fine. I've been sick lately, I don't think I'll ever be well again, and Daddy gets breakfast and I get dinner."

Mr. Goodie entered the room and told me about McNess home products and said, "I say, give everybody the same opportunity. Don't favor me because I'm a Negro."

I suggested that if blacks wanted to move into Watertown today, there would still be a problem of finding housing. Mr. Goodie said, "Oh, it's *there*, honey, no doubt about it. When I was trying to find a house I later found out that there was a mutual agreement among real estate people not to sell. I found this out because a certain person in one of the real estate offices told me. But like I say, I don't let this bother me, no reason why I should. If I was to let racial digs bother me, I'd go around with a frown all the time. Why should I stir up something? If I could stir it up and do some good, okay. But like these protesters, they stir up trouble and that's all. All this destruction on campus and we the taxpayers have to pay the bill."

I asked what he thought of Father Groppi.

"I'll tell you frankly, I've always been a very strong supporter of Father Groppi, but there again, honey, he's made mistakes. But at the same time, I consider the good he did overshadows that. In other words, we're not supposed to be perfect. He had to be beautiful. He did it from the heart. He was talking for the good of mankind. He didn't have anything to gain personally and I think he was all right. Now that Martin Luther King. All these protests and sit-ins started from him. And his nonviolent way was fine if they'd kept it that way. But no man's perfect."

I asked if he thought the world has changed a lot lately, in the last five, ten years.

"People are changing," Walt Goodie said. "There's so much frustration going on. Too much selfishness in the world. If the people would go back to the Bible and do what Jesus said. What religion are you? Catholic?"

I raised my eyebrows and said, Jewish?

Mr. Goodie slapped me on the knee. "Oh, *that's* all right. You're God's chosen people!" He continued, "In the morning, you leave for school with a song in your heart and someone looks at you with a frown and you don't think much of it. Then, you're still feeling happy and you see someone else with a frown. And someone else. And pretty soon you don't feel very good anymore. That's what's happening in the world. That Vietnam situation. I think that's caused more trouble in the world than anything else. And why not? Who would want to send their son over? Kids these days are afraid to turn nineteen. And people are disgusted but the thing they gotta do is go back to the Bible. And you're Jewish, Lynn, that's okay. The prophets in the Old Testament said exactly what's happening today. So what the people got to do is go back to the Bible."

We talked about Detroit a little; they had been all over the country in vaudeville and he remembered a lot about it. Before I left, an hour and forty-five minutes after I'd walked in, they took my name and address in Detroit and I told them I'd visit them again. They said, "You *do* that."

January

I

The beginning of January saw more controversy. On January 10, 1968, an underground newspaper in Madison, *Connections*, ran an article by Jeff Yablon titled, "watertown! whither, oh wither?" It began,

There is a city in Wisconsin where a bitter fight is being waged for open housing. People involved in the movement are subject to obscene telephone calls, not too subtle threats of losing their jobs, and even less subtle threats on their lives. A clergyman is leading the struggle. An underground newspaper has started.

After discussing *Soul* and surveillance, it went on,

A fair housing ordinance in Watertown would not hurt anyone; the two Negroes don't even want to move. It would just be a gesture. But it is an unwanted gesture. The City Council recently voted to purchase riot equipment, including ten rifles with sniperscopes. I interviewed the part-time mayor and asked him why this type of gun was ordered. "Well," he said, "you never know when some guy'll climb up in a church tower like in Texas and start shooting at people." He added that the police sometimes go elsewhere. "Ten of our boys were in Madison for the riot." He does not expect too much trouble from the two aged Negroes. "We've always had a Negro shoeshiner in Watertown," he said proudly. . . .

Movements to fire the pastor are occasionally spoken of, but the high-schoolers are strongly behind him. Armed with full voting rights (anyone who has been confirmed can vote in the United Church of Christ) they are too formidable to fight in a showdown vote.

The article concluded:

Still, these teenagers, some of whom march with Groppi are shaking up this quiet town with NAACP sweatshirts, "Black is Beautiful, Baby!" emblazoned on the back. As the pastor says, "We're scaring the Hell out of them."

Perhaps as important as the article itself were the pictures accompanying it: George Washington, looking somber, reading a pamphlet to smirking children, an old drawing entitled, "I will bathe once a day," a Boy Scout with all his decorations, a woman sitting high on a pedestal, and perhaps most importantly, a drawing titled "Does Censorship Really Work?" The drawing was of a naked woman, her legs widely spread to the reader and a sign covered her crotch saying "Censored."

Bill Guyer told me he thought the article was the straw that really broke the camel's back. He thought that Kromholz had distributed the article.

The Bentzins referred to it as obscene and absolutely pornographic and also told me that Kromholz had distributed copies of the newspaper.

Peg Buckland told me she thought Kromholz wrote the article.

Kathy Isaacson told me she sat in on part of the interview with Kromholz. "It was very dull," she said. "I don't see how they got such a rabble-rousing article out of it. It was yellow journalism is what it was."

Frank Isaacson said, "It was a really bad thing. Kromholz didn't like it either. It was really crummy."

Mrs. Isaacson mentioned that what was happening to Al Kromholz was a lot more obscene than those pictures. "In those terms, it was an acceptably dramatic presentation."

Sydney McQuoid told me the kids thought it was really hilarious because of the pictures. "Not really accurate, but funny."

Chuck Yeomans said he thought it was pretty bad and he felt the pictures were pornographic. He told me it was passed around the congregation. I asked him who passed it around and he said he didn't want to say with the tape recorder on. Afterwards he said it was Mike Bentzin.

There was more bad press coverage. On January 12, an article by Rudy Pelecky appeared on the front page of the *Capital Times*. The article dealt with open housing and the phone threats received by Kromholz, by another active minister, Del Miller, and by students. While its tone was not as bombastic as the article in *Connections*, it could hardly be called favorable publicity.

The following week the second issue of *Soul* was published. Far more important than the issue itself was an incident that occurred while *Soul* was being written in the church. Sydney McQuoid said, "Well, we had gone up there to write *Soul*, not to type it off or anything, and Mrs. Schmutzler [a congregation member, and Oscar Schmutzler, Sr.'s daughter-in-law] came in and asked what we were doing and we said we were writing *Soul*, and she got really really upset. She went out crying or something. And we were quite upset because we had the feeling she would call someone. So I called Mrs. Kromholz first, and she got very upset and said, 'Well, call your father,' because Al wasn't in town. He was in Milwaukee. So I called my father and he said, 'Now take it easy and I'll be down in a little bit.' Well, in the meantime Bentzin came in and he started kinda throwing his weight around.

He told us to get out, that we had no right to be there. And we retorted with things like, 'Well, we're members of the church, we have just as much right to be here as you do.'"

Did you have permission?

"Yeah," she said, "we had permission. The Church Council had told us that we could write a copy and then we would present it to them and they would look at it. And they had said if it was okay, then they would publish it. Well, we were gonna *try* and get their okay without any changes in it. Otherwise we'd run it off somewhere else.

"So, he came and he got really really angry and he started yelling at us. He started pointing at Ruth Richter who happened to not be a member of our church. 'What is she doing? She doesn't have any right to be here.' We said, 'God's house is open to everybody.' I remember right before he left, when he couldn't get us out, I think it was Kathy [Smith] who said something and he said something and she retorted, 'You're being very unchristian.' Well, these things really seemed to get to him.

"So he left and brought Mr. Guyer up and Mr. Guyer says if we can just please leave and he'd talk it out with Mr. Bentzin and Mr. Jaedecke [who had also come]. And they convinced Mr. Bentzin that we did have a right to be there but he — Guyer — said, 'Why don't you leave for awhile, just to cool off?'

"So we left and we didn't really hear too much what was going on. I could see my father was visibly very upset about it, but he controlled himself, he didn't say anything to Bentzin, but when he left Bentzin made some fine remark and my father said real cheerfully, 'Well, we'll see you in church Sunday morning.' And that was a cut at him because he hadn't been to church in probably two months. And then we just left and we came back after awhile but then we were too upset and we left. All I remember is that it was visibly very upsetting because I remember just about being in tears, and

Ruth Richter *was* in tears. We didn't do it in front of them because we didn't want them to see it."

Mayor Bentzin remembered the incident also. "Once they were back in the church office on Saturday and Donna Schmutzler went upstairs to get something and saw them. By then the Board had said no go, they couldn't use the church, and they smarted off to her and she went and called me and I said what can I do? I'm not on the Board. She said somebody's got to get them out of there, so I tried to get Paul Jaedecke, of Paul's Dress Shop, and someone else. And finally Paul said, 'Okay, I'll go if you'll go with me.' And I said, 'Look, I'm not on the Board, I don't want to get mixed in with all this,' but he wouldn't go unless I did, so I went."

Mr. Bentzin told me the next in a gruff voice. "I said, 'Who gave you permission to be down here? You'd better get out *right* now, and *don't* get smart. You'd better get out.'

"They made some more wisecracks but they got out. And when I walked out there was McQuoid, you know the guy, chunky and always looking mad. He was standing outside, wouldn't come in to defend them. And he just started to leave without saying a word and I told him, 'Listen, McQuoid, don't think I can't take you.' You know he's the wrestling coach and thirty years younger. 'One more crack and I'll take you.' But he just turned and left. These kids left and never came back. Imagine the guts of these kids after they'd been told by the Board not to be in there."

11

Peg Buckland, a long-time church member in her early sixties and youthful looking, told me how she had spent her day the day we spoke. "I got up and I ate my breakfast and I didn't wash the dishes, I put them in the sink, and I had several telephone calls to make because I am in charge of — we're going to have a parade of homes to raise money for the hospital and I'm the chairman of the committee so I had several calls to make about that. Then I had a call from a woman, my friend whose husband's in Madison, and she called to say that he could come home tomorrow. So we made arrangements for that. Then I left and went to the florist and bought some pansies and went to the cemetery and planted them on my husband's grave. Then I came home and grabbed a cheese sandwich and a glass of milk, and had a call from my neighbor up on the hill, 'Are you going downtown?' She's been sick, she's a lonely woman and she wanted to get to Third and Main so she could take the bus out to her friend in the seventh ward. So I said, 'I have to be at the hospital for a meeting at 1:30 but if I can get you *right* away, I'll ride you out there.' So I did. So I *just* made it to the hospital at 1:30 and I came home at a quarter to four and opened my front door and there I saw my neighbor's yellow car sitting out in front. And I hadn't talked to her for a couple days so I phoned her and talked to her until you rang the bell."

Discussing Al Kromholz, Mrs. Buckland said, "I think when he first came we were all enthusiastic about him, and about his wife. Then it seemed that he became more interested in affairs away from the church. The thing that got me the most upset was when he got involved in this bulletin that he edited, or that the underground kids edited. This group of seven kids that met mornings. And apparently they edited this thing, *Soul*. Especially the one that was so greatly — illustrated. Really I thought — there isn't anything to be said about it."

I said I thought the illustrated one was *Connections*.

"Oh yes, maybe that one's *Connections*. And then there was an article in that magazine about our church. Yes, that was upsetting to me, I didn't really think that our church had any business in that magazine. I didn't quite see the connection. Well, sure these things are on the market all the time, but I didn't really think it gave our church much reverence when there was this article in there which undoubtedly was written by him, and some of the pictures were pretty — "

We went back to the beginning.

"Well, when he first came I liked him," Mrs. Buckland said. "I thought he was friendly. I remember one time, soon after he came he went calling on Mrs. Yeomans [Chuck Yeomans' mother], out in the country. She was an older lady, and I happened to go there and to call with a friend of mine, and he was real cute that day. She served tea, and he had tea, and we bantered back and forth, and you know, I kind of liked him and I thought he was boyish, and you know, kind of — attractive."

Discussing Father Groppi she said, "The thing that irritates me is that he was *marching*, and that destruction was happening because he was marching. Maybe he has drawn more attention to the problem, I don't know. But I can't approve of that way of getting at the problem. Through marching. Gosh, everybody's got something they'd like to have. Well, suppose everybody goes out and — everything's relative. If they were using some of their time that they're marching, they're wasting their shoe leather and they're really not *learning* anything. If they wanted to learn I would think they'd best spend their time in some kind of a training program.

"But marching, I just can't see where marching gets you. And I don't really think I'm, you know — " she paused, "bigoted. I want these people to have a chance but I just don't think this is the way to help them. To me, it's just like trying to raise a child that — they *want* something, but everybody can't have everything they want. Like those ADC marchers that marched through Gimbel's and the Boston Store and took clothes off the — well, that was last summer. The welfare mothers, who had the many illegitimate children, well, they got marching and then they walked through the Boston Store and Gimbel's and they would just take *arms* full of clothes off the racks and throw them on the floor, or take them out, or steal them, or anything. I just can't approve of this. To me this just doesn't make good sense."

I asked what reason Al Kromholz gave for marching with Father Groppi.

"I don't know," she said. "He didn't give any to me. Just that he wanted to exhibit his interest in civil rights movement, I suppose. Well, I've no objection to Father Groppi, I mean as a man, whether he's Catholic or what, that makes no difference to me, but I think if you were being paid by Hevi-Duti and you went marching with the strikers over at Durant, it might — this is the sort of thing it seemed to me was just out of line. He was being paid by the church, this is where his job was, and he was every place else but the church.

"I would just say that he really *got* to be a smart aleck. When I first knew him, I didn't think that he was such a smart aleck. Now whether he developed this to a greater extent or I didn't see it at first, I don't know. But we got so that we didn't go to church. I understand this one service where he and McQuoid ran down the aisle, screeched or something. It sounded just horrible. They were trying to bring out some point but I was not there and I don't know enough about it. Somebody that you interview maybe could clue you in on that. Seems what they did was so disrespectful and really quite removed from anything to do with the church. I don't mean that I don't think the church should be concerned — I think the church should be concerned about people.

"I mean, I certainly don't think we can stay apart from the world, the church has to be involved to a *degree*, but I still think if they don't stick to their job of, well, teaching about God, well then what's the difference? You might as well go to the Rotary Club. I'm not saying the church shouldn't be socially involved. But it has to have the other. The Gospel is important. Now some people might like to go to hear about problems but I go to hear the Gospel. To get my battery recharged.

"So many of his sermons were *really* not Bible-based. They were just civil rights or something like that. I mean, I just think his whole attitude was so — irritating. You'd get so irritated that you'd hardly — I mean, he wanted to *tell* you, you *do* what I say. But he didn't have any practical suggestions of doing. I mean it was just very vague. But I think it was more his *method* of presentation than the subject matter sometimes, although somebody can tell you about this awful sermon where they raced up and down the aisles. As I say, we got so we didn't bother to go. I mean it just felt like a waste of time. Rather stay home and read a book or listen to some other man on television or something.

"Oh my husband just practically blew a gasket, he was so furious at him. And so we didn't go, I'm sure, for three or four months. And we didn't pledge either. Well I mean how else could you combat it? If he was telling all this stuff you didn't want to hear, well why go and listen?

"I felt sorry for his family and everything, but after all, that was his responsibility, not ours. I will be just so interested to know someday, I hope I do know, whatever becomes of him. But I think so many of these protesters and marchers and all, they just want *attention*. I just think they're pseudo-sophisticates and they just think they've got *all* the answers and good heavens, thousands and millions of other people have been trying for the answers for a long time."

Did she remember her reaction to the first issue of *Soul?*

"Well, I didn't see it for such a long time till after it had been so greatly talked about. The thing that I did feel in talking to people, that he would get these kids, I mean he would tell them they don't need to do what their parents say, they should do what *they* say. And this caused among people I knew quite a bit of dissension in families. Because who's this young pipsqueak to tell the kids, pay no attention to what your parents say? I myself didn't have any particular run-ins with Alan. I mean I didn't have much of anything to do with him, really. Except, of course, I certainly voted against him when the time came.

"And I still think he will live to realize that he

made some pretty bad mistakes here. I mean, if he wants to be a social worker, well, that's fine. One meeting we had, they told him that. They said there's nothing wrong with being a social worker but you're trying to serve two masters. He could use his social work in his ministry, sure, but not to the extent that he was trying to use it."

Mrs. Buckland affirmed that she had helped to get more people at the meeting that took place in November. I asked if she could tell me what happened at that meeting.

"Well, first of all he was going to set up a tape, and Mr. Bentzin objected, and so they pulled the tape off. Well, it was just frank discussion, dialogue, back and forth between the two. But Mr. Parker was there and he's given to being — he gets *very* worked up and of course he said, 'He's a Communist, he's a Communist.' Well this really wasn't fitting to the situation. But, well, it was just the opposite of a mutual admiration society."

Did he answer questions?

"Not very adequately, no," Mrs. Buckland said. "We felt that really nothing much had been gained — I mean, when he called the meeting we thought that he was sincerely interested in putting forth an effort to get this thing lined up. I don't mean that he was going to give all the way or we were going to give all the way, but that we understand each other better. But I don't think so, I think that he was predisposed to what was going to be, and it was going to be that way or else."

What was he predisposed toward having?

"To just doing what he wanted to do about any question. I mean if he wanted to be gone to Milwaukee and march with Father Groppi, he felt that the church had no business to stop this."

Did anything good ever come out of the meeting?

"Not that I ever heard of, no. I think that our, my husband was living then, our reaction was that we were just a little bit more disgusted with him than we ever had been. He was sort of like a smart aleck."

Referring to when Mrs. Buckland said it wasn't fitting to the situation to call Alan Kromholz a Communist, I asked if in fact she thought he probably was.

"Well," she said, "I wouldn't be surprised. I mean he was extremely close to this Fries who they say is a very active Communist. And certainly his attitudes and actions would make you think that he was."

Fries or Kromholz?

"Kromholz."

I asked if she could be more specific.

"Well, I don't know of anything he *did* that was Communistic. He started this Human Relations Council, I didn't see anything wrong about that. I'm interested in that sort of thing but I was so irritated at him that I wouldn't have thought of going. But I'm afraid I can't be more specific than that. 'Course we had a tendency to *name* people for various things and don't have foundations. I couldn't say to him, 'I think you're a Communist.'"

I asked how she would define a Communist.

"How would I define a Communist? Well — a radical thinker and actor who wants to bring about change with revolution, rather than evolution. One day I said to him, it might have been after that meeting, 'Al, you're a great guy and I like you,' you couldn't help but like him, I mean he had a kind of attractive personality, I said, 'You can't change the world overnight. People have been working at it for years and years. It's a long hard pull.' When I said that to him I'm sure he couldn't have cared less. It just went in one ear and out the other. I'm sure he didn't pay any attention to it."

Was she upset over his not making sick calls?

"Yes. I work at the hospital once a week and he would *fly* in and *fly* out. And I'm sure he couldn't have — I was never sick so I couldn't — I felt awfully sorry for his wife. She would come sometimes and be crying, you could just tell, her eyes were — so sad looking. And then all these anonymous phone calls they had, I don't know how she stood it. I don't think she was as radical as he was. She probably just went along."

I asked what she thought of what happened with open housing.

"Well, I don't think anything is accomplished by — he made such a stink in the community about open housing. I never feel anything is accomplished this way. You can't win people to your cause if you're going to antagonize them, in my book. And this is exactly what he was doing. If you want to win friends and influence people, I think you gotta be nice to them, and try to win them over. Well, that I think would have passed without much furore if it hadn't been for the way he went about it. Oh, he went up to the City Council, hollered around, made a big show and created a lot of ill will. Well, yes, I agree that there should be an open housing ordinance. But as I say, I think that would have passed with no trouble if he hadn't made such a racket. No matter what he did, he seemed to get a split in the wrong place. Now, whether he realized he did this, or whether this was just his childish ways, I don't know."

Did she remember any opinion she had at the time about buying riot guns?

"No, except that we'd better prepare ourselves. The riots were that summer, so I suppose it was the handwriting on the wall. They thought they should be prepared."

Why did she think those riots happened?

"I don't know," Peg Buckland said. "Because I think outside instigators went in and started it. I don't think half the people, when Groppi came through here, when they went to Madison, I think all those people think, ooh, great, a parade, let's go along. And black people are very emotional and they probably just get all worked up and half the time, I don't think they know what they're parading for."

I asked if she thought the church takes too active a role in things like that today.

"Well," she said. "Yes. I don't know that clergy-men need to be leading a parade really. I think they're better off spending their time and energy helping individual people. I know it's a slow process but — each one help one, that sort of thing to me would have greater possibilities of helping more people, eventually. Than the way they *try* to do it. The riots, I can't see that anything is accomplished except destruction of property. And if they'd spend this money *helping* the people, instead of breaking things down. That's one thing I think with Kromholz, a friend of mine made this — she said her criticism was, well, here was this man who comes into our community, he wants to tear everything apart, but he has nothing to put in its place. Which I think, really, makes the most sense."

We turned to more general topics.

"You young people are too idealistic," Mrs. Buckland said. "You can't change everything overnight. Education is the most important thing. We have to teach these people to want to have a job, have to teach them how to spend their money. But you can't change innate intelligence."

I said that some people today say that people are poor *because* of the system. I asked what she thought of that argument.

"Well, I don't think much of that. I think they have to be educated."

I said the argument is that they've been kept poor.

She replied, "Oh, I think either they don't want to work, or they're lazy, or they're — stupid. I mean they can't help their mental ability. They can try to improve it but I mean if it's limited, it's limited. People from that environment I guess generally have more limited mental ability than others. Partly because of lack of food and things, as well as their heredity.

"I *know* that some of these people live in squalor and it gets terrible and they shouldn't live that way, but they have to be taught to pick up their orange peelings, or, maybe they don't have orange peelings but they did over in India where we were. And *oh* that was awful, you'd just trip over them all strewn all — and I read the other day that they have 79 million rats in Taiwan. Well, I don't wonder, they just throw their food all over every place. But I think when we try to work with these people you do take for granted that they know a lot of things and of course they *don't*. Their growing period has been — they just grow, and I mean it's going to take a long time for them to learn a great many things that we just take for granted in our way of living."

Mrs. Buckland told me she likes David Lawrence's column in *U.S. News and World Report*. I asked who she thought makes sense politically.

"Oh, I don't know. I think they're all terrible. I think McCarthy would have been good. I voted for Nixon, I can't say I'm too pleased with him, I mean I don't see why he has to have a house in California, that all costs money. Couldn't he have a house a little closer to Washington? And I don't think he needed to double his salary."

What did she think of our going into Cambodia?

Very slowly and measuredly Peg Buckland said, "I don't think I'm for it. On the other hand, I very well remember a woman who came to talk a number of years ago, right after the Second World War. And she had lived there [eastern Europe] and she went back again after the Communists had taken over, and she told about the situation there. And this was so vivid and so real and she knew what she was talking about because her parents were still there. At the time they didn't even give her name because she was afraid.

"So if the Communists are going to take over southeast Asia, I mean, to me it's so confusing. I don't think this is right. But, on the other hand, who are we to go and say, well look, we'll fix everything up. I just think the United States is wrong in that. Anymore than if I knew my neighbors were fighting in their house, well, it would hardly be my business to go and say, now look, you don't do this, you stop this. They'd say well go home and mind your own business. And I think that probably this is what people maybe should tell us."

So you kind of liked McCarthy? I asked.

"Yes, I thought he would have been all right."

He was for getting out, I said.

"Yeah. Well, does anybody really want war? I can't conceive how they do. Nobody *wants* it. But on the other hand, do we have to — I don't know, I don't know. I mean, it's wrong, there's no doubt about it, it's very wrong, I as well as anybody else thinks it's very wrong but maybe the Administration knows more than we do. I hope they do. I hope they know more than I do. But I, I just, I don't know what's right. But on the other hand we don't want the Communists moving in either."

From a previous visit with Mrs. Buckland, I thought I had remembered her saying that she thought Kromholz deserved the phone calls he received. I was not absolutely sure she had said this so I asked her again.

She said, "I just know I heard about them. I don't know anything about them. I can't imagine who would make them. I think probably, maybe people not even in the church. That was terrible too. I mean if they wouldn't say it to his face, well, then I think they shouldn't have done it by phone. I don't *approve* of anonymous calls or anonymous letters or anything like that. But I would say again that I thought he had them coming. He *deserved* them really."

Was the worst thing that he was away from the congregation and marching — that kind of thing? I asked.

"No. I think that the worst thing — to me the thing that was the most detrimental to the church was his concentration on these seven kids and I didn't think that was fair that the other kids who might be somewhat interested in a different program were completely out of it. I mean they had no consideration. And then this underground business, not underground business but underhanded business of telling young people 'Pay no attention to what your parents say.' To me this was the most serious.

"We *had* to be rid of him, I think. The church had to be rid of him, the town had to be rid of him, and for his own sake — he may learn to know that as he matures I think. He's *very* immature."

Why did he *have* to go?

"Well, because he was creating a split. I mean the church was falling apart, the attendance was terrible, and his *standing* in the community. I mean you look to a minister, I would think, as somebody that would be a leader and a respected man and conduct himself so. But he just — he didn't seem to care what he did."

III

Father Vincent Thilman, of St. Bernard's Catholic Church, is in his sixties and has been actively involved in social action for many years. In the Catholic Church, however, the congregation cannot vote to remove the priest. Father Thilman said, "Al and I think a good deal alike on a lot of social questions. I think we just kind of hit it off, I don't even remember when we met, but in talking I think we kind of realized we were kindred spirits in a sense. So both of us at different times had been working with high school students on this sort of thing, getting them interested in something, as I call it, something beyond the Rock River. And these would be matters of race questions, migrant workers, and later on, the war, and things like that. And I think Al and I thought pretty much alike on these things. And yet I could see that Al was making more enemies than he was keeping friends, within the framework of his church I'm talking about, hmm? And I don't think this is necessarily right, but I used to keep telling him, I said, 'Al, I know where you want the people, I appreciate that, but you have to take them where they are and see if you can bring them along an inch at a time.' Now I don't follow my own philosophy, see? I got all kinds of people here who would just as soon have me moved, see? Although there are a great number of people that worked with Al and are real good friends of mine, hmm? There's a lot of wonderful people in this community. I'm not going to count and see which way it is, fifty percent for or against, you understand.

"So Al, I think, was so zealous and so convinced about this whole business so that, as I say, in a way he was defeating himself because he wasn't gaining the strength that was necessary to help bring around the end product *if* we were going to do it with the present adult congregation, you see, hmm? Now, that doesn't mean that's wrong, you understand, because maybe it takes awhile and a few martyrs to get, and in the meanwhile the young people are growing up, you see. He had the younger people, there's no two ways about it, you see, hmm?

"One of the things I think that griped people considerable and that's Al with the high school kids, helped them with a little newspaper that was kind of provocative, but it was something that it was good for the people to be provoked about, hmm? And it was run off at their church, you see. I think unbeknownst to some people, I think it was run off here a couple times, but anyway — " Father Thilman laughed. "So some of them thought he was corrupting their youth with this thing, when actually it was true Christian Gospel teaching applied to problems that there are in the world, hmm?

Speaking of his own church, Father Thilman told me that he had supported the migrant workers' grape boycott with a number of other priests and that the owner of the local radio station had sent him a letter saying he abhorred the idea of the church getting involved in questions like this. With the letter he sent Father Thilman a copy of *The Manion Forum*, so Father Thilman could know the other side.

"*The Manion Forum*, it's a radio program and this was a write-up of the thing. Manion was a fellow who loved the Constitution unless it's for something that he dislikes. In this program, Manion was interviewing a man by the name of Gonzales, and it turns out to be the Gonzales who for two years lied to the Feds, claiming that he was not paid by the growers to break the strike, see? So I had this newspaper clipping about how he was [paid to break the strike], and then he vanished and took the records with him and so forth. And that's supposed to be the other side. Well, that kind of stuff is what you get day in, day out, on our local radio. And so it kind of perpetuates the thinking that is here in the first place, of don't disturb the water, all these stories of injustice must be fabricated or something."

Father Thilman said some of the people on his parish council resigned "because our people don't like our stand on race questions and things of this sort. And poor spiritual moral leadership, you understand. I don't know what that refers to, except that I suppose that had reference to the idea of not teaching children the traditional Watertownian [pronounced Water-tone-ian] doctrine. That's the only thing I can fathom that it referred to. I didn't remember shooting any policemen or raping any women downtown so — but that's weathered. And the leaders of it kind of lost face as it turned out. But there's a partial rift still going on."

Getting back to Kromholz Father Thilman said, "Al was a lot younger and had a lot more energy than I have, you see, and so probably in a sense I gave in. But I don't think it was really that. I think it was a matter of realizing, 'Well, look, you're only making things worse. They know your convictions already, there's no use rubbing it in.' That sort of thing, you see, hmm? I was trying to get him to — you can still present the things but in not such a rambunctious way that you turn so many people off."

I asked if Al Kromholz ever heeded that.

"Well, I don't know. Like I say, I considered myself a good friend of Al's and I liked him very much and that hasn't ceased or stopped, you understand, hmm? On occasions I would say to myself, well, I wished he'd a done it this way, in order to maybe get more friends for the cause rather than just say how strongly you feel about the cause."

Why did he do it the way he did?

"I think it's Al. I think it's just his personality. I don't know whether that's a fair judgment, but that's the way I feel about it. And of course a lot of these things you only learn by going through them. I got a million stories about how I used to start and then say, no, we gotta do it the subversive way. That word isn't the right word, because it sounds dangerous, you see. At least it's underhanded. Nevertheless, it's the way we got the Catholic schools in South Bend opened to Negroes.

"Well, what we used was we realized what's-his-name on the east side and Dolan on the west side never would let each other get ahead of each other on anything. Well, once that come to mind, we picked out the most likely one and got him to say okay, and then casually got invited to supper to the other fellow's place and mentioned it, and before long we got five parishes all with their doors open.

"One time in a tough all-Catholic neighborhood a friend of mine was gonna sell his house to one of my parishioners [who was black] and it was all quite Catholic neighborhood, see, so I told him, 'Charlie, I know what I'm going to do.' So I found out the day that they were moving the furniture. The toughs were going to be there. So I parked a half a block away with three servers, dressed up in Catholic surplice with a cross and two candles and we laid the furniture into that house. And I never blessed a house so much in my life. See, you always bless just the inside. We went all around the outside, see. Well, the whole thing came off. The people came to be friends with their Catholic neighbors. So, as I say, trickery is dandy, you see, because people have their foibles and what not, and you can use them. And I suppose maybe this is what I was trying to say to Al, well, don't be so blunt about the thing. Let's maneuver a little, catch them when they're off guard, that sort of thing. But I don't know if the gang that was solid against him would have changed their mind, it's hard to say."

I asked why the town reacted so violently against Kromholz.

"I, I don't know all the ins and outs of it," Father Thilman said. "One of the things was that the Mayor was part of the congregation, and he had a lot of friends. That was at least one item. And see, it was right around the time of the open housing thing and I suppose Al was more apostolic than the rest of us and going around batting his head against people who wouldn't have their heads batted against."

Did he think Kromholz had neglected his sick calls?

"Oh, I think that was a dodge, that sick call business. I think that was an excuse for people to use who didn't like him. I get the same guff. We'll always go when somebody calls, but we don't feel like we have to go down to the hospital every single day, and some people don't like that. But I think that was only an excuse for people to be against him without appearing to be against him for the cause they were against him."

I asked why it is so threatening to them that a man has a different opinion.

"Well, logically, it shouldn't be but — it's a strange little town." He laughed. "I don't know, it's so much status quo, as I say, status quo. No vision beyond the Rock River. Put that together and you see why should we have an open housing ordinance? There's no Negroes living here. Not realizing of course that it's a slap in the face to every Negro in the state. They might as well put up a bill-board out at the entrance of town, all the way around, 'We Don't Like Negroes.' Same thing. And to think that Negroes don't know that Watertown refused an ordinance — it's a lack of awareness."

What do you think will happen in this country?

"I don't know," Father Thilman said. "I think we'll be lucky if we get off without having a revolution of some sort. I don't think the patience can keep — well, now look, tonight's newspaper, I just looked at it. I think it's Mississippi, governor of state announces that the investigation shows that the police officers were in their rights in shooting these Jackson students. *Well.* Look at that Black Panther thing in Chicago. Glow-ry be, how much can a group of people take, hmm? Before it used to be just insult, you see, they don't service you at the counter, they don't take you to the hospital, they don't take you in their schools, or you're not wanted in our church, okay, these were insults, but glow-ry be, today there's no safety anymore, physical safety.

"And so as I say, now a lot of our young people in the country are looking through all the façade and saying, 'Well, that's what we're doing,' and people are yelling, well, our beloved Constitution. But it doesn't apply to these people, you see, hmm? I mean, all these lovers of the Constitution, they love it when it's for the things *they* like, hmm? So as I say, the young people are seeing through this more and more. And I don't think it's true that the only ones seeing through it are the activists. I think an awful lot of kids are, and I'm not against an activist. What I'm talking about is a lot of kids don't happen to join the groups but are still thinking the same way nevertheless, hmm? And I think there's the hope."

IV

The teenagers working on *Soul* were by no means the only teens actively trying to improve their life in the community. Starting in the summer of 1967 a group began to work actively for the establishment of a coffee house in Watertown. In the middle of January a long battle to find a home for the coffee house came to a close with the donation of facilities above a department store. Alan Kromholz was one of the adults who worked on the effort.

The idea for a coffee house, according to its first president, Steve Schaefer, came from Father Green of St. Bernard's Catholic Church and a good friend of Steve's, Gordie Miller. They had been planning to set up a coffee house for some time when Father Green was transferred. Steve said that Gordie then got some other priests and ministers together to discuss the idea of a coffee house. It was at this time that Gordie, a few years older than Steve, talked to him one night when Steve was drunk.

Steve, who was a junior in high school in 1967–68, said, "So Gordie told me about this whole thing, and I guess I was drunk, and I was laughing. I thought, I could *not* imagine, like I was telling you how we came from the grease crowd, I could not imagine the guys that I hung around with getting up on a stage with a microphone and saying, 'We've been taking a lot of shit down at high school, let's talk about this and that.' I thought this will *never* happen. The only thing is gonna happen is somebody's gonna say, 'I got a case of beer out in the car, if anybody wants to buy it — ' That's the only thing I could imagine. So anyway, I didn't want to have anything to do with it, I was terribly messed up, really messed up, didn't know where my head was or anything."

In general or just that night? I asked.

"In general, just in general," Steve said. "I was just really messed up. And it was a whole reaction to my parents, it was a reaction to school, it was a reaction to my religion [Catholic], it was a reaction to *everybody*. I was just messed up.

"I was a sophomore [then], and I was messed up and I couldn't make anything matter and this seemed like it might. Just sort of in the back of my mind. I thought — I wasn't dumb like the greasers were. I had an alienation of the greasers because I'd go to take a test and I'd like knock it off and the greasers would always have a hard time with it and they'd say, 'How'd you do?' and I'd say, 'All right,' and they'd say, 'Oh, you bastard, you got a good mark on it.' And I felt alienated because I wasn't dumb. Well, that was one thing where I had some satisfaction.

"So anyway, Gordie got this thing going and I was sort of reading up on it and it sort of made some sense and I thought maybe it'll work. So I started working on it. And Gordie had this meeting with these ministers and they talked about it and thought it would be a good idea, but it was just a beginning, just talk. And it just so happened that Al was doing somewhat of the same thing in his church. Gordie found out about this, Gordie went and talked to Al, Gordie came back to me and said, 'I got the perfect guy for you, Al Kromholz.' I didn't know who the hell he was. So we sat down and talked about this and he got us a lot of literature on it, a couple books on it."

Al did?

"Yeah. And he had a lot of stuff and he started to break it down, like saying if you're going to have a group like this you're going to have to have certain committees. And like you're going to need a committee for entertainment, refreshments, for this a that, a secretary-treasurer. He started breaking it down and he was the one who helped us a lot with organization, organizational tact, and with the idea of what a coffee house was. But that was something nobody could really help us out with. That was so intangible we had to work it out and make it relevant for Watertown.

"So then they had a meeting with adults and the adults got ahold of this movie called, 'You Want to Build a Coffee House.' And there were about twenty-five kids at this meeting, four adults. This took place in the summer, in July. And all of a sudden I was chairman. I don't know how, it just," Steve snapped his fingers, "happened. They asked me a question about a heater, that's it, and I knew how much a heater cost, and that's the way it all started.

"Then we started looking for a building. The next thing was a building, it was money and it was like we were right up against a wall, we didn't know where to start. And nobody even knew anything about a coffee house except Gordie. And a couple of ministers did but they didn't work on it so much. And I was supposed to be chairman and I didn't know *shit* about it, exactly what a coffee house was. I knew how to build things, and as I found out in the course of that year, I had some leadership ability, and therefore I knew I could lead and I know I could build, and I knew I could paint, and stuff like that. But I didn't know what I was doing it for.

"And oh, the next couple of meetings about seven kids would show up for every single meeting. So we said, okay you guys are the Coffee House Board. And then Burn quit because his mother put too much pressure on him and Barb Carlson quit because her parents just thought we were all a bunch of Communists. And then from then on it was just five. None of us knew *what* we were interested in, or *why* we were, we were just doing it.

"So we started meeting and we didn't know what we were meeting about, but we knew we needed a building, and then we were lucky we had a few adults that knew exactly what it took to get a building. So we went and talked to a guy by the name of Archie Loeb, who runs Loeb Salvage. And he had an old building which was up next to Chase's Bar. It was an old dump, you could see outside from inside and inside from outside, it was just falling apart. Well, we said we wanted it.

"So we got one Saturday, it was just a matter we had to get something generated, so we had about thirty kids, we went out and cleaned up the place. It was just *terrible*. I mean we picked up the rocks, raked the grass, mowed the lawn, flipped around and everything, picked up all the bottles, and hauled them out to the dump.

"And then the next week Archie Loeb found out it was for the Coffee House and he found a bunch of kids were running it, he got pressured. Adults in the community *pressured* him. 'What are you letting these damn kids do? You know Kromholz, he's the one going to Milwaukee, he's involved in this.' And Kromholz was involved in it. 'And what are you letting these damn kids do?' And he's got a business that depends on public relations, he's in the junk business, and he has to have people. And he just said, 'I'm sorry, I can't work it.'

"So what we had then was about fifty kids who wanted to work on this thing and nothing to do, no place to go. So we looked around, and we just — *lucked* out. We went to *every* place. In fact, one night, it was so *stupid,* we were so desperate, we had twenty kids. Three kids, we went down to city directory and we went to every single vacant building in Watertown. We went *everywhere.* We'd go in groups of three and walk up and down the street and find a vacant building, write it down, and call up the guy, see if we couldn't get ahold of it. And then they'd say, 'What do you want it for?' 'We want it for a coffee house.' And the response, people would just — " Steve made a noise like a machine gun, "tuuum, tuuum, tuuum. They just wouldn't get this. They kept saying, 'Well, what adults are running this?' We'd say well Al Kromholz, Jim Shaw — "

I asked why they used Kromholz's name. Wasn't there someone else's name they could have used?

"Well, see, we didn't realize," Steve said. "You have to understand that we were politically inept. We knew *nothing* about politics. We knew nothing about Al. And we could see no reason why what Al was doing would have been bad at that point, at the beginning. Well, then maybe after three months you start figuring maybe we ought to use Jim Shaw's name, and then we got the veterinarian Doc Wagner to work with us, and a guy by the name of Gene Bolt came along eventually. And then we started using these names of course after we finally learned maybe that had something to do with it. We got some face people."

I asked him what role Sydney McQuoid played in the Coffee House. Sydney had told me she was the only person really involved in both *Soul* and the Coffee House.

"At that point Syd was marching with Father Groppi and nothing in Watertown made any sense, see?

Watertown was beyond saving, so she would go to Milwaukee. So Syd wasn't involved in it. In fact, Syd never was involved in the Coffee House until after it was pretty well set up, because she kept knocking it. And then she was involved in *Soul*. And then her and I had somewhat of a conflict. Because see, well, I was boneheaded for one thing and I was a new-hatched leader, that's one thing I'll admit to right now, that I made a lot of mistakes, and I was overly dominant in a lot of things, and I did like the limelight and sometimes I used it to my advantage a little bit. Maybe more than I know, I don't know. But I made a lot of mistakes at this time and Syd was aware of every mistake that I made, and made it known."

I asked what he thought of *Soul*.

"Well," Steve said, "*Soul* came out and it didn't impress me at all. I thought it was — there were a few articles which were good but unfortunately it wasn't relevant for Watertown. It didn't make any sense to Watertown. It came on too strong, I thought. These are all my personal opinions.

"And the problem was that there was a correlation between the Coffee House — see, we were just in our beginning stages and *Soul* came out. And they thought that the Coffee House was putting out *Soul*. And so we disavowed ourselves from *Soul*. I got a very nice letter back from the Board of Education, a very nice letter back from the Chamber of Commerce, a very nice letter back from the Rotarians.

"So when we disavowed *Soul*, Syd took this as a personal attack, she took this as us not supporting the youth movement, not supporting civil rights, not supporting the anti-war thing, not supporting anything. And in essence it was just a matter of saving our own throats because we thought that if we got something going that we would have substance, whereas a newspaper you can throw together anywhere with five kids and print off and sell. But a coffee house involved maybe five hundred kids. And we tried our best to rationalize it and still I stick to that rationalization. I might have been scared then, I don't know, I just know it had to be done because if we were going to get tied up with *Soul* then we were going to be shot."

What were your political views at that time?

"You mean my own personal political views? Ignorant. Then I was against violence. I was against marching too, which is really strange, now that I think about it. I was against this mass movement thing and I think the reason I was against it was because I was finding success in being able to work around this thing. I was finding success in being able to brown-nose enough to get things done without having to march. And possibly this was sorta saying, well listen, if I can do it, other people can do it."

What did you think of Groppi?

"I thought he was very good. I liked what he was saying."

Did you think Groppi was cool even when you were against marching?

"Uh hm. Because I listened to him on TV and I said he's got a point."

Steve continued about the Coffee House. "Well we finally got a place. And it was just luck, pure luck, I can't imagine how it happened. So we found out that the Masons, the Rainbow Girls and the Masons, anyway, they had a place above Fischer's Department Store, where the Coffee House is now, and they moved out because they built a new place. So we went and we talked to Karl [Fischer] and surprisingly enough, Karl was receptive to the idea. I don't really know why Karl was, but he was. And he's taken too much shit from us, I don't know why he did it. He's put himself out on the limb so many times for us, but he's always been such a — reasonable guy about it.

"The adults took care of most of the talking. We went over to talk to Karl but it was mostly adults. Nobody listens to a fifteen-, sixteen-year-old kid. Talking about something this extensive. So the adults talked to him, they finally got it, and I'll never forget, we had to have a meeting. After the meeting [with Fischer] Al says, 'Steve, come up here and sit down.' He says, 'Well, we got a place for you.' I was ecstatic, of course. 'We got three conditions, though.'"

You weren't even up there when they did all this? I asked.

"No, I wasn't in on this when they got Karl's place, because we just figured, hell, why should we go and just hamper the thing being stupid little kids, and a lot of the adults were willing to take this responsibility. It was great. Al says, 'You're going to have to have an adult up there all the time you're open.'

"And I said, 'No, no, no, you can't.'

"And he said, 'Well it's a matter of getting a place or not.'

"So I said, 'All right, I suppose.' Because we were all psyched up on this idea of youth responsibility. Well, anyway that was set and when it would be open and exactly how clean it would be and that stuff."

Steve told me that someone who knew a lot about coffee houses came up and told him exactly how to do theirs, where to put the stage, what colors to use, what kind of curtains. Steve said he exploded. "It took me awhile to understand there are people who know more than I do. So anyway, we did it that way, and it turned out absolutely fantastic. It was absolutely great. There was no other way, it was perfect. It took us until I think it was March 21 was the day that we opened. We could have crammed it but we wanted everybody to get involved in it, as many people as we could. So we worked on this, not like pushing it. Mark Hazenow and I worked, I think if we got paid a penny an hour for every hour we spent on that place, both of us would be millionaires right now. We would go up there and both of us work until maybe eleven at night setting stuff up so that the next day when the kids would come up, they would have something to do.

"And we needed money and we'd have an occasional dance and we'd collect money and we'd get some donations. So it was getting to the point where it was starting to shape up, starting to really look nice. And there were so many kids working on it. Oh, fantastic, kids were starting to come up there all the time to work on this. I think they just wanted something to do. And we really had a great time.

"And finally March 21 we opened with a big adult night and we served coffee and we were nice to everybody and we made some more money 'cause we set up a jar 'donate' and we got more money 'cause we need like a water heater. And then after we had impressed the adults quite thoroughly that this was an all right thing, we thought that we should start moving into what we wanted."

Steve told me he got to know the president of a coffee house in Madison quite well and that they had a "main dream" to set up a chain of coffee houses in southeastern Wisconsin and to coordinate them with a newspaper or rotate speakers and maybe have some political force. "But it never materialized," Steve Schaefer said. "And I don't think it ever could, really to be honest, I don't think it ever could."

Steve then told me that Al Kromholz got kicked off the Coffee House Board. "Oh, this is a little coy politics. 'All right, boys and girls, sit down, we want to talk to you. Well, as you know, we've been having a lot of trouble with Al —'"

Who was saying that? I interrupted.

"Jim Shaw, Doc Wagner. Two men we really respected. And they said, 'Well, Al's been having a lot of trouble with his church and we also know he's been working with Groppi, that he's been marching and he's been neglecting his church duties. And besides that, we have nothing against Al, you know, we think he's a fine man, but he's getting this political image in Watertown and people won't listen to him anymore and there's some talk about asking him to leave the church, and we really think if you want to get this organization off the ground, that you should really — you really don't need him anyway.' And they snowed this into us and they voted to kick him off. Something that one of the Board members now regrets. He's not in Watertown anymore but about a year after that, we sat down and talked about the whole thing, and he said he was very sorry about it but he didn't know Al at the time. Anyways, so they convinced us that that was the thing to do. We all of a sudden were shocked into the reality that we were not running this thing anymore."

I asked Steve if he could remember when this was.

"I remember it was cold and mushy out. 'Cause I remember walking by the church one day and feeling guilty as hell, and I looked up at the church."

Did he know how Kromholz felt about it?

"Yeah. He was quite pissed off. He felt quite let down, like we just took the rug out from under him. And rightly so. And he never trusted me after that. He took it out on me and I didn't know. I really hate to plead innocence but I think I got kind of a shirt job, when I look back on it now. But at the point I was rationalizing, constantly rationalizing this thing, yeah, I guess they're right, I guess we've got to do it. I thought we had to."

Steve told me about some of the activities during the Coffee House's first season, which ran from March 1968 until the following fall. "We'd have a band or something like that and once in a while we'd have discussions. We got a speaker from Boys' School which was very, very great. We had the Wisconsin Draft Resistance up there, which was good too. It just scared the hell out of everybody. And now I look back on it, it's trivia. They were so conservative it's sickening, like they were cop-out liberals. But at that point everybody was," Steve sucked in his breath, his eyes wide, "*Aaaaaah*. They thought the world's coming to an end. Kromholz spoke, and the Mayor spoke.

"And now looking back on it I think this vast movement of having controversy, of having speakers, having kids, was what generated the group that tried to destroy us. And there was a core group that was doing this. I think this started after Kromholz. There was a group that never wanted us up there and we didn't fear that group at all."

Who were those people?

"I don't know, I wish I did know. But anyway, after Al was up there, it was so coy, there would be a god-damned inspector up there two or three times out of no-where. Or the janitor. I think the goddamned janitor was getting paid off by somebody, because he musta collected cigarette butts for three months, then he'd hand them in to Karl, then he'd threaten to quit work. So he was using that pressure on us. Okay, he didn't quit. And I talked to Karl and he said there were some people who were coming up and telling him they wouldn't shop there any-more if he didn't get us out of there."

Steve told me that rumors spread that they were selling and manufacturing dope, that they had Com-munist material up there and that they were trying to set up a revolutionary movement. "So there were these ru-mors all the time and they'd eventually get back to me through my dentist, who's an *ass*. He *believed* them, that we were selling dope. I'd sit there with my mouth open, he'd keep hitting me with all this stuff and I had all this shit in my mouth and I couldn't back myself up."

Al Kromholz spoke at the Coffee House shortly after he was dismissed from his church in May. Mayor Bentzin spoke there later in the summer. I asked Steve what the speeches had been like.

"We had Al come up," Steve said, "and Al talked about the civil rights problem. We wanted him up there because we wanted some controversy up there. This whole thing was based on controversy. We wanted some-body to talk about civil rights, which was important. The war wasn't really that important then. Or we didn't think so. So anyway, Al came up and he talked about this, and there were — like the place was packed. That was great.

"Well, the one thing when Al was up there, I think I was so busy working because I don't remember being there that much at Al's thing. I don't remember if it was a clogged-up toilet or some very trivial thing that I didn't grab the whole thing, but I was there for some of it. Since I knew Al real well and I really knew what he was going to talk about, I figured it was my job to keep things cool — so between running around and telling people to shut up and fixing the toilet and stuff like that I didn't get much of his speech.

"But people listened, a lot, listened quite a bit and asked questions, lots of questions were asked. And most of it, Al was getting to the point where they were starting to ask him just trivia about the civil rights thing, about violence, most of them came up with this idea of violence. And there were a couple of adults who got up and left, got pissed off and left. But there weren't enough adults up there, which is unfortunate. Because the adults who were up there, I don't know how they really could have been too uptight because, well the kids were with him."

I cut in, Did you think that what he said was radical?

"No," Steve said. "The only time was when he had a hard time answering about violence. Which is something that now I can really relate to but at that point everything seemed that non-violence was the only answer. He was ahead of King you might say and when King denounced violence — but like he was ahead of him and he had a hard time answering about violence. That was the only thing that hassled me. And I was just ecstatic after it was over because it was the most people that had ever sat there, the most people that had ever been involved in a discussion. There were some kids that asked questions that I didn't know knew how to speak, they'd never said anything to anybody. It was fantastic, I really thought it was great. It was packed and it was a very good discussion. But did we get the shit!"

Who gave you the shit?

"It's hard to say. It just came. See, the adults weren't ascared of us, they really weren't ascared of us individually. Collectively they might have been. But they'd sit down and say, 'Well we don't think that you little boys and girls should be listening to Al Kromholz.' That idea. But they would really give the adults a hard time, so they just jumped all over it. They didn't think that it was right that people should be allowed to go up there and influence kids. Their big thing was this idea influence. So we countered this by having the Mayor up there. It was a long time after Al, in fact.

"Bentzin's was something else. I don't know who the hell Bentzin thought he was talking to. See, when you had a discussion with Al or something like that, he talked to you, not at you, or down to you. And Bentzin, and usually just talking to adults like that, they usually talk down to you like a bunch of little kids, where Al always gave us such a feeling of respectability, that we were human beings and that we in some way had a right to make a decision. Where Bentzin didn't. Bentzin got up there and talked, he had it all written out, he had a sheet of paper and he went just like this, read the whole damn thing. It was, 'When I was a boy many years ago.' I'm not kidding, 'We used to have little clubhouses down by the —' "

Is that because he didn't respect you or because he just didn't know how to speak?

"No, he could have come on different. The whole emphasis of it was, when *I* was a boy we used to have little clubhouses down by the river, and this is a little clubhouse down by the river too in my eyes. See maybe he didn't understand what it was but he related it to a very trivial situation and that pissed me off for one thing.

"Anyway he goes through this thing and he just didn't understand his audience, he didn't understand the Coffee House, and he thought it was just a little club and he made some funnies like, well we never used to let girls into our clubhouses. He got done with this and gave the proverbial slap on the back that youth has the power tomorrow but you're not getting any today, that idea. So he went on and it was just sickening, he went through this thing page by page by page by page.

"Mr. Bentzin always thought I was a pretty good egg, he knew my mother real well, he knew my father real well, and I shook his hand and I smiled and I took his shit when I had to. Like I'd say, 'Yes, sir, may I help you, may I walk you around?' and this thing to him meant a lot, this outward show of respect. Like asking if I could take his coat, 'Would you like to see the place? Could I give you a cup of coffee?' This thing meant so much to him. I thought why the hell alienate him on that point?

"So anyway we had the discussion and afterwards it was sort of getting very heated. And what really surprised the hell out of him was he thought we were just going to talk about 'Oh, we like you, Mayor,' but we weren't. We were concerned about the issues of Watertown. We were concerned why recreation was getting cut, why they were building these damn lights up here and they weren't putting any money into the park facilities, why they weren't building a recreation building, why the YAC, which is the Youth Activity Center, was having trouble getting dances. Why it was underneath the Police Department.

"And then we went into this idea of race, of why the City Council had voted down open housing law. And there were some kids that were sharp on it and said, 'Why didn't you show tokenism that you supported open housing?' 'Oh we don't need to and the federal and the state will take care of it.' 'Could it possibly be that you don't want to?' And he just wasn't prepared for that. And I still to this day don't think he could answer some of those questions that were put in front of him. He was just uptight and finally he just quit. And he got to the point where he wanted to get out so bad, a fire truck went by, he stepped off the podium, walked over to the window to see the fire truck go by. And this was during the discussion, when it was supposed to be going on. He finally, he just cut it, he just left. And he was very very uptight.

He always put on this air of being so damn sure of himself, when he walked out of there he was so uptight he was shaking, he was very nervous. And he kept reassuring me that he thought it was a good place. 'I think this is really a great place Steve, really a good place.'"

Mayor Bentzin remembered his speech at the Coffee House. "After we got rid of Kromholz on the Board the kids asked me to speak, and of course they didn't think I would. But I did, I had a prepared speech and after that the kids started giving me the time. They didn't think I'd come and they were laying for me. Like they'd ask me questions that really have nothing to do with Watertown. That night they asked me questions like why don't kids ever come back to Watertown? Well, I was mayor at the time and none of my three sons live here now. I said that, my three sons, and they all laughed. It's the name of a book or something. Well, for some things you just can't live in Watertown. Now, doing what my boys are doing, they couldn't live in Watertown."

I asked who was there.

"Who was there? Well, Steve Schaefer was there, he was president and they were lucky that such a responsible person was. And his parents were there that night, I think. They were often there. They wouldn't dare run it [the Coffee House] without adults there. And Barb van de Hoogt was there, and that's where I met that colored girl I was telling you about. That girl from Milwaukee that they're paying her way through school, I think business school. And she was a nice looking colored girl. Real nice looking and they had her all dressed up nice."

Mrs. Bentzin said, "They kept asking us, 'What are we going to do for the youth? What are you going to do for us?' I don't know why someone should be doing something all the time."

Bentzin said, "'I'm sure the city gives you every opportunity,' I said to them. I gave them some dry wall for the Coffee House that we had around here and someone else gave them some money. There were no problems after they got rid of Kromholz at the Coffee House."

Steve Schaefer told me that after Al Kromholz got fired and Del Miller, the minister of the sister United Church of Christ, resigned under pressure, and then two other clergymen were forced to leave, "all of a sudden I started getting a picture of how this whole thing is held together, the spit that holds this thing together. It's held together by fear. Watertown has a lot of rich people, and a lot of poor people, and the big people got their money because they played the establishment's game. And it's sort of like a miniature America, you might say. They convinced the smaller people that their way is the only way and that anybody who intrudes on that is Communist or bad, or they will not be able to get their dough if they don't go on according to the way the big boys want it. And also a lot of people are on fixed incomes and any type of tax increase is really gonna hurt them. But the rich people in this town, they really run the whole show, and you find out there's so many small people, face people like Bentzin, who's a face man. I don't really think he has power on his own. A few industrialists backed him, or people who had dough. I don't think we'll really ever find out."

v

The Congregational Church's annual meeting was held on January 24. New officers were elected and Bernard Garlid replaced Bill Guyer as church moderator. A resolution that the church go on record as being in favor of fair housing legislation covering all housing in Watertown was tabled by a 47 to 32 vote.

In the Annual Report presented to the congregation, the Finance Committee chairman submitted that "the amount pledged this year is over $7,000 less than the amount pledged last year." The total pledged was a little over $16,000 as compared to over $23,000 the previous year. Also in the Annual Report was an itemized list of budget cuts totaling almost $5,000 to accommodate the loss in pledges.

A resolution to create a committee to study ground rules regarding the dissemination of church publicity was accepted by vote of the congregation. This committee was the result of dissatisfaction with the annual report of the Church Council in which the following standards set by the Council appeared: "That the pastor use extreme discretion and as far as possible clear with the Council any inserts of a controversial nature in the Sunday bulletin," and "No material of controversial or political nature may be published, except by the pastor, that is not approved by the proper board, or by the Church Council." The second part dated back to a resolution passed at the November Church Council meeting after the publication of *Soul*. The committee was told to report back to the congregation within six weeks.

Frank Isaacson was on committee. Referring to the fact that he had been on a committee in late November, he said, "I don't know why the hell it is I got on all these committees. I'm not really that articulate and didn't represent anybody. I think, well, they were surprised that anybody would say anything. Maybe they liked to have somebody there who was reasonably polite. Reasonably. I wasn't really obnoxious about it. It wasn't really too unpleasant."

Referring to the committee created at the annual meeting, he said, "I had the same problem there. And I don't know, maybe it's me. I get hung up on semantics and I get terribly concerned about how something is written. I mean maybe people don't even see those little differences. Like 'can' rather than 'should.' It turns out there are certain key sentences in everything.

"I think that Frater, in retrospect, he sort of bull-dogged right through, pushed the thing right through. It seems to me, and maybe I put too much importance on what I had to do with these things, but it seemed to me that nobody else really gave a damn."

Speaking of the issue of censorship, Isaacson said, "They did object to the principle and they said, well, maybe it can be a temporary thing. Someone else said, well, it doesn't seem like a very nice thing to do. And I objected strenuously to it, as a matter of principle. That's why I went to see Gordon [Frater] at night, privately. Because I didn't think that was a fair way to do it. He said, 'Well, sometimes you have to do things that aren't — that you don't like to do.' He said, 'You know, sometimes you have to decide if it's worth[while].' "

After some tense meetings the committee recommended a somewhat milder set of standards concerning publicity.

VI

Bob and Jean Bertling are a couple in their thirties. Bob Bertling works for the telephone company and at the annual meeting was elected to the Diaconate, the board that takes care of the everyday running of the church.

"The night after I was elected to the Diaconate," Bob Bertling said, "like I say, I didn't have too much to do with the church, but I went over to his [Kromholz's] house and I talked to him and I kinda used the excuse, and it was, of being a new member of the board. I wanted to visit and become acquainted with him because we were going to work more closely, and I tried without being too obnoxious or being too much of a, what would you call it? pushy, I guess, to kind of clue him in the way people felt.

"And I got the impression he figured the hell with them, phooey, if they don't like what I'm doing, that's tough. And I came home that night, I was very discouraged, I told Jean, 'He's like a little kid, he doesn't even know what you're trying to tell him. You could almost come out and hit him right smack in the face with a cold fish. He doesn't understand it.

"When I got on that Diaconate, boy, I used to keep hearing this word, 'the problem,' and it started here," Bob Bertling pointed to his ankles, "and every meeting I'd go to it'd get a little higher, and pretty soon it went right up to here." He pointed to his neck. "And one night Bausch came out with, he said, 'Well, you know we have this problem.' And I said, "Now lookit, I've been here for four or five meetings,' I said, 'what's the problem?'

" 'Well, you know what the problem is.'

"So I says, 'No, I don't.'

"And he said, 'Well, we'll talk about that sometime later on,' and all kinds of circling and I wouldn't let him go. I says, 'Let's talk about it now.' So finally we got it out and boy, I'll tell you it was just like opening a floodgate. You should have heard those people talk, had all this stuff in them for a year, all the things they didn't like, but they wouldn't say a word. Because they're Christian people, and Christian people will not talk about their minister or do anything to — lower the church's image in their eyes.

"Well, it took two months or better, two or three meetings, and boy, everybody was telling each other their feelings at that Diaconate meeting. But this is what happens all the time, people just won't tell you what they feel or what they think. Until the very last minute. And maybe looking back in a different perspective, if people might have gone to Kromholz earlier and been honest with him, maybe he would have been a different kind of person. But, he was their minister, so — "

We went back to the beginning. I asked if people liked the minister at first.

Jean Bertling said, "I kinda liked him and I got a kick out of him. He'd call and he had all these ideas, and I went along with them and I — "

"I would really have to say that we weren't too active in the church other than going there Sundays," Bob Bertling cut in. "Jean was. Jean was the first to become involved. See, I was in Cub Scouts pretty much — "

Mrs. Bertling said, "I think I brought it home while I was on the Mission Board, stuff that Alan had said. I'd come home and tell you, and you'd almost fall off your chair." She laughed. "Then they asked you to be a deacon."

Bertling replied, "He was probably, I would have to say, he was probably the *first* one to kinda have me to kinda put it into my way of thinking, *questioning* just what the mission of the churches are for. He was the one that brought it out. To me. As to what the mission of the church was. This business about whether a minister has to make a choice, what's his choice going to be? Some place as a missionary worker or some place as an individual who's supposed to minister to his local congregation, and then after he's accomplished that responsibility, then if he has any extra time, fine, who cares? That's the way I see it.

"Well, I don't think Mr. Kromholz was doing that, I don't think he was ministering to his congregation. You see, and he had a tremendous knack, the reason it took two years," Bertling laughed, "Jean and I talked about this, he never did anything really that alienated a tremendous amount of people. He used to — *pick*, and he'd knock a few off each time he went into one of his programs, and pretty soon when he dropped the last boat and the wave just kinda washed about, that's what it amounted to."

Bertling discussed the difference between the Congregational Church and the Evangelical and Reformed Church. The Congregational Church is a free church where you're responsible to yourself and to your God. It is up to the individual as an individual to accept the responsibility that goes along with Christianity. But there are others who say, " 'Establish a goal for me so I can be a good Christian.' And I'm not saying they do this intentionally but it's like figure this out for me so I don't have to think too hard, see? Give me a direction. And I think this is what Reverend Kromholz was too, see, because Kromholz was Evangelical and Reformed and they were a lot more close-knit church with their goals.

"And that's another thing I was just thinking about,

Reverend Kromholz was immature. [You have to] realize that there are factions in a church and no matter how you cut it you're going to have them. You gotta kinda work with them, both sides, to accomplish anything. This is what Kromholz has never learned to this day, I don't think. He thought they were mad at him personally. He thought we were picking on him for the things he was doing, not how he was doing them, not how he was maintaining his job here but because of the individual personal things he was doing. He took it as an individual, as a person, that people were mad at him because of his stand on civil rights. All the way through this thing he thought he was being ousted, picked on, whatever you want to call it, for the stands he took on these things, and this wasn't the case at all."

I said tentatively, It was because he was neglecting —

Bertling laughed. "How deep do you want to go over this?"

I'd like to, I said.

Bertling then proceeded to tell me about the group meeting that was held on November 17 which they did not attend because Mrs. Bertling's father had an operation in Kenosha that day. Bertling said they had reached a consensus "that he cool it and people try to be a little bit more liberal. They kinda solved the problem." Bertling went on to tell me that Kromholz had made a lot of promises that he didn't keep, when his wife cut in.

"I had heard there were some *hotheads* at this meeting, *really* some nasty things were said to Alan."

"I don't know about that," Bertling said.

"*Oh,* Bob."

"Oh, they accused him of being a Communist and all that stuff, see?" Bertling said.

"Some people were really cutting him up," Jean Bertling said.

"But this is what you run into, you know you got factions in churches," he said.

"I think maybe that hurt him, though."

"Maybe it did, maybe it didn't," Bertling said.

I asked if they thought Kromholz was a Communist.

Bertling said, "No man who goes to a seminary and believes and works for God as a missionary and really takes a beating, he can be a lot of other things but he certainly can't be a Communist."

"I think that's just a dirty name," Jean Bertling said.

"And you have a group of people in town who did a lot of investigating," Bertling said. "And that he was seen with unruly characters or I don't know — "

"Yeah, that's right," Mrs. Bertling said. "That's where it came out. See, I think this is where some of this, I remember a couple of older ladies saying this, 'Do you think he's really a Communist?' and I said, 'Now that isn't a nice thing to say, he might have his faults but — " She was really kinda worried there. 'I've heard this,' she said, 'I've heard this around a lot.' And here's a gal seventy."

Who was doing the investigating? I asked.

Bertling said, "Oh in general, people who have a — I'll tell you one thing, I'll tell you what happened. This is what really set me off kind of wondering about Alan." Bertling then told me that when he was at Kromholz's house they talked about environment and growing up and Kromholz told him he had a hard time and had to carry water and chop wood to keep the furnace going. "I knew Al was from Merrill," Bertling said, "and one day a fellow came out here from Madison and we got to talking and he's gonna retire in three or four years and I said what are you going to do and he said, 'I'm thinking of going back to Merrill where my brother is, and where I was born.' "

Bertling told me that he asked the man if he knew the Kromholzes and he said he did and when Bertling asked him if they were kind of poor he said they weren't poor at all, that they probably had it better than the average in Merrill. According to Bertling, the man said, " 'What? Carry water? What would he have to carry water a mile for?' So then I kinda started to wonder too, a little bit. 'Course this just kinda smoothed it out. This had nothing to do with anything in general and in fact it didn't even enter my mind except right now when I just got to talking to you. But."

Jean Bertling said, "I felt bad that when he left town, not that we asked him to terminate but some people must have treated him — "

"If a man — " Bertling started to say.

She continued. "I mean, I never knew and I never talked to Alan afterwards about it but he was supposed to have received phone calls and letters."

"Oh, he did, he took a beating," Bertling said.

"I could *never* understand that," said Jean Bertling.

He said, " 'Cause his wife was a real, a real fine person, I think. Friendly, warm, when they first came out here. She left, I think she had an awful lot of questions in her mind about people. 'Cause he was called up and threatened."

"I can't imagine," she said, "I can't imagine anybody in our church, I just can't. But then, on the other hand, you never know. I can imagine them being a little brisk, talking to him, but I can't imagine threatening, telling him he better be careful."

"They were a good bit more vicious than that," he said.

I asked what open housing had to do with the whole controversy.

"Open housing?" Bertling said. "No, that was very inconsequential. They had a special meeting one time to pass a resolution on open housing and there was very little debate and very little discussion and somebody made the motion to table it, and that's where it is today. That was all, there wasn't anything, that was the *smallest* part of it. All the church boards refused to take a stand on it and they passed it right up to the congregational meeting, and at that meeting, like I say, there was very little discussion about it, nobody said hardly boo, hi, or anything else. Somebody stood up, made a motion to table it, which was probably all set up beforehand.

"Let me clarify one thing, and that is when people took the stand that they weren't going to vote on an open housing law, they weren't taking a stand against open housing, they were taking a stand against the fact that they didn't think it was *necessary* to pass an open housing law, in Watertown, or any place, because this right and freedom is supposedly guaranteed. This was the same tack and the same approach that a lot of cities and counties took at the same time."

No law was needed because it's guaranteed?

"It should be guaranteed, right? And if it isn't guaranteed, then it really isn't a legal problem, it's a Christian problem, and this is something then that the church ought to be able to do with their people as individuals, not pass a law for the whole city or the whole state or the whole federal government to live by. And now you get into the whole faction of conservatives against liberals. Liberals don't think that. Liberals feel as though you have to pass all these laws to make people live by them. The federal government has to kind of watch over you, and I just, I just can't go that route.

"We had another situation with the *Soul* paper. It could have been a fine thing. After all it was written by a group of I would say intelligent young people, but I think they weren't the most worldly in the world. And some of the things they put in the paper had a very bad effect for the program they were actually trying to foster, and that was to be able to express themselves. The understanding I had was he read these papers before they were printed and condoned them, see?"

"That's where a good adult leader could have worked well," Jean Bertling said, "could have stopped a little bit of it. We could still have had a paper, but with the right leadership. If he had been more, I mean he was supposed to have read them, he admitted he had gone over them with them, he didn't say they'd gone out without his knowledge, so you can assume that he proofread them or what have you."

"Kromholz," Bob Bertling said, "is not the only individual like this, and this is the thing that I think is rather distracting, it kinda subtracts from the whole problem, to categorize *him* as the problem, 'cause he isn't. I think the whole church in this country today is kinda running scared. I don't think the people in the churches and the people in theology and the people in the seminaries, I don't really think they know what they're doing. I think they know they failed in a lot of cases, not being too successful. I think they measure in weight you'd have to say, but they miss maybe in volume. We got a tremendous number of Christians running around this world, maybe they're not real heavy with programs and stuff, but I've got a firm belief that if each individual was a good Christian, you wouldn't have to worry about all these big programs that it takes masses of people to accomplish. The word is 'shock,' the word is 'shock,' this is the new tactic. *Shock* the Christian.

"And here's another thing too, now how this leaked out — you know what *Connections* is? It gets kinda dirty. All of a sudden a great big article comes in this underground newspaper in Madison about what a savior Reverend Kromholz was and what a dirty bunch of creeps there are in the city of Watertown, and everyone figured, now how the hell did they get ahold of that? Come to find out, he's leaking press releases out to the people in Madison see? And there's no doubt in my mind that his motive at that time was he wanted a job in the association somehow or another. He was looking for something better where he could carry, where he could move and carry on more of his policies."

I asked if the Bertlings knew anything about the city's purchase of guns. He hazarded a guess.

"I don't think they bought the guns for here," Bertling said. "I think they bought them in Watertown's name for Milwaukee. First the rifles weren't right and they had to send them back and then the rifles came and they were right but the scopes were wrong and they had to change that, and to me that indicates that they didn't know what they wanted here and were ordering for somewhere else. Like Milwaukee for riots." Bertling laughed heartily, remembering a story in the *Capital Times,* in which Mayor Bentzin said that the rifles were for a sniper in a church tower. Bertling thought that was very indicative of the Mayor's brand of humor.

In the spring Al Kromholz proposed having a film festival and according to Jean Bertling all the chairmen of all the boards got together with Kromholz to discuss it. "I think it was the one time I got kind of disgusted when I was talking to him. Otherwise I never really said a whole lot, although I wanted to, just to tell him how I felt, because I felt that was a fair thing to do because Bob had done it. I just couldn't. We thought we would like to see one of the films, we did see one and we asked Alan, no, we didn't like it and couldn't see how it — oh, it was kinda goofy about shooting people, how you give a little child a gun and show him how much fun it is to shoot at the targets and next thing he's going to be out killing people. It was against killing. Well, there's really nothing wrong with it, it was just kind of a goofy film. We thought, why, just why? Because we felt, I'm sure it wouldn't have bothered the kids too much, but things were flying around town as it was, and what if the parents of these kids — found out we had this Communistic film about war propaganda, how we, as a country, love war and the whole bit. So we told him not to. Have a film festival, there's some excellent films I'm sure the kids would like to watch, why this particular one?" Jean Bertling said that what really got her mad was that after the board chairmen had told Kromholz not to show the film she heard he then showed it at the Coffee House.

She went on, "I just felt so bad on our board though, there was a nice gal, and she liked our church, and she worked on the Mission Board, too many years really, but she wasn't so, oh in her early fifties and her husband had passed away and she cried once at our meeting, it was about two months later, when this talk about Alan was coming out, and she said, 'He just never came to my house, I needed him so badly and he just never came to visit me. He came to the funeral.' He took the funeral for her, and he should have visited her."

What was her name?

"It doesn't matter really, except that she just felt crushed. I think it was the first time I had really heard of someone being neglected. We didn't need him at the time but she just couldn't get him, he just wouldn't come visit. And from then on you'd hear dribble by bit."

"He never made the hospital," Bertling said.

"I mean, people felt bad," she said.

He said, "People who had been shut in, in the church, didn't have communion for about a year."

Bob Bertling then told me what none of Kromholz's supporters knew and what no one else had told me. He told me how Kromholz was fired.

"I think what happened was there was about five of us who got together at different places at different times," Bertling said, "to discuss just what we were going to do, just what kind of course we were going to take because, and the real basis for this was the fact that nobody knew how to go about it, see? According to our constitution, it says nothing in there about how to get rid of a minister. When did we start meeting? It took a good three or four months to do, to — this committee wasn't formed to get rid of him. This committee wasn't formed to get rid of Kromholz. In fact, this wasn't a committee. This was just a group of individuals who got together and we were trying to decide whether it would be best for us to take the step back to Congregationalism, at that point. And we didn't want to get involved in this because we knew he had supporters, and we didn't want to start tearing this whole thing apart, see. And people consistently kept coming up to us and saying, maybe it wasn't always nice, 'When the hell you gonna get rid of him?' just like that, and it was getting to a point when you couldn't see anybody from church without them saying, 'Get him out, get him out,' and they were really getting vehement. So, we in the middle of the river, we figured, okay, that's the way she's gonna be, so we drew up a resolution stating because of this, this, and this that we feel it better that the church and Reverend Kromholz dissolve their partnership or something like that. It was a very nicely worded resolution. See, we had another problem here. This is what really took so long, for us to really figure out how we were going to do this particular thing, because we knew there was going to be a lot of emotion and a lot of hot feelings and everything else. And so we had to be very careful the way we worded the resolution because we didn't want to give any specific reasons that people could point to and say okay, give me dates, times, and places, and so we didn't really word it specifically. We did this to eliminate emotion and argument.

"See a minister has to decide in this day and age whether he's going to play the politics game or the religion game. He's gotta get out of one and into the other, or into one and out of the other, or something. They don't mix. If they're going to try to mix it, they're going to lose the church.

"Unless someone can change the whole system, you can't go out and try to accomplish and *do* a lot of these things that these people are talking about, because our whole society just isn't set up for this kind of thing, see. And if you want to have what we're having now, a lot of anarchy and mobs and everything like that, that's what you're going to end up with. Because people certainly feel frustrated, I feel frustrated about a lot of things that go on in this city, but I think if you feel frustrated enough then it's time to go out and organize groups and petition and go about the thing properly. Not go charging into someplace without any support.

"We all have the same goals, the same things, equality, racial justice, but the question is, how do we get there? What do we do? And I think that's a factor of maturing, sure, I know I can't change it. I'd *like* to but I can't individually and because I'm not immature, I'm not frustrated about it."

Jean Bertling said, "But you *are* frustrated."

"Well, yes, I'm frustrated but not *so* frustrated." At this point Bertling asked me how old I was and then said, "Oh, there's only seventeen years difference." He said when he was at Madison in the early fifties they thought the same as young people today, "and felt the same things, and questioned it, but that was as far as we went. We fought with our parents as much as kids today, so it wasn't fear, but we had one thing going for us that the kids today don't seem to have, which is respect for people older than yourselves. Today this isn't the case. Today a lot of young people feel as though the older generation's completely botched it, and they're the recipients of all these bad little things, just like we were the recipients of the Depression and so forth.

"Those kids aren't mad at the war. That's a tool, a vehicle for their emotions. If there was no war, they'd have something else they'd be mad at. I think that a lot of these kids are lost, they have really no direction to go. Because they've been fed so much liberalistic *crud* in colleges in the last ten to fifteen years, that it's just pathetic. I think they're presenting problems to young people that people for generations have been trying to solve, and they're frustrating these kids because they can't solve them."

I asked if Kromholz could have taken the positions he did and still have survived, had his approach been different.

"Certainly he could," Bob Bertling said, "because people moving voluntarily in the directions of social change is kind of doubtful in my mind, but they all want to in the end. Who wants to see riots, who wants to see all the young people in the country alienated from the system or whatever you want to call it, who wants to see somebody be able to hold a man down economically and spiritually because he's a different color? Nobody wants to see these things. I shouldn't say that, there are some people that do, but by and large I think the majority of people in this country, even as strict, as conservative a city as Watertown is, I think the majority of people realize it's going to come, it's going to have to come, and they want to do it as painlessly as possible. Now painless to each person has its own cut-off point, and that is where the hurt comes."

So if Reverend Kromholz had made his sick calls, and done what he was supposed to, and also done the other — I began.

"He couldn't have done it. Because he doesn't have the personality for it," he said.

I said, No, let's say another man, had he managed to do both —

"Do you think a man could?" Jean Bertling asked.

"I'll tell you something," Bob Bertling said, "as far as talking about the church. Let's face it, being a Christian, a good Christian, is the big problem to solve. I think there's only been one man born, and we all know what happened to him. People don't take this politics, church business lightly."

VII

I went back to talk with Jean Bertling since she had not said much when I spoke with both her and her husband. She was wearing tennis shoes and had dirt on her knees from gardening. Three and a half years before we discussed it, Jean Bertling had written an article in the March 1967 *Church Chimes*. The article began,

How do you explain an exciting day full of interesting and thought-provoking ideas thrown at a Mrs. Average Housewife in just a few short paragraphs? I'll try though! After attending the Legislative Seminar in Madison, March 1, I feel ever so much better informed on state problems. Christian political responsibility is not optional, I assure you, but a necessity to all of us. We must, and may I emphasize "must," become more aware of what goes on day by day in all phases of our government.

I showed her the article and asked how she felt about it now.

"Yeah," she said, "I wrote just what I was supposed to write. It was a very interesting thing that I'd gone to, and I suppose I was [more enthusiastic] at the time. More so than I am — As I say, I still feel that the church can be involved, but they have to be careful. More than Bob feels [it should be involved]. He probably sees further into it than I do but — "

We discussed poverty in America. I said I wondered how we can get rid of it.

"Will we ever get rid of it?" Jean Bertling asked. "What would it be like if everybody was even? I mean it'd be so strange, unfathomable, I mean, how do you understand that?"

I said, I guess it's a question of how much should you just give to people and how much you just let them work their way out of it.

"But they claim some of them just can't," she said. "And I keep thinking of the poor child that has a stigma right away when he goes to school and he's behind and he never learns really how to read and he stays in junior high and he gets out and he never really gets a job and just keeps going downhill all the time. It's hard for *me* to understand. You'd think they'd be able to catch them in kindergarten or grade school and everyone should have a good education. And then you shouldn't have to have the big problem of having to help them later, but that's probably impossible. Whether just to hand out more welfare, you know, how far do you go? 'Cause I've heard of some of them getting some tremendous checks, but then, how do I know? I *hear* this and I don't go over and talk to them, and how they spend their money foolishly, go to the grocery store and buy stuff that I probably wouldn't buy."

I said that a lot of people say the system keeps people down.

"On purpose? It's true that there's always been poverty and I'm sure that we just can't — If we could just erase it some magical way, it'd be like magic all right. I can't imagine. I'm sure more money could be spent, if it were spent properly. I think in time, through education, I suppose. I don't know if you've heard about Sesame Street, I think stuff like this is great. I mean maybe it's such a tiny little bit if these kids can just begin to want to learn and start learning equally. 'Course I talk to my cynical husband, and he says just how many jobs are there? And people live longer, more medical discoveries, is this the law of nature? It sounds terribly cruel, but it's just like with animals. You want to think we're better than they are, and of course we are, but how can it ever?" She laughed. "It would just be fantastic. Or if everyone just had two children, and if everything just went — what book is it I read awhile back with the test tube babies and the whole bit? *Brave New World.* That kind of jazz. It would have to be like that, wouldn't it? I'm sorry, I really — and yet I laugh, it's just like pollution. I know I shouldn't use some of the detergents I use because they pollute the water and yet, I haven't used the enzymes. And like spray cans, and a lot of waste paper, and canned this or bottled that. Am I ready?"

I said, "What if someone suggested that the only way to get rid of poverty in this country would be to raise federal taxes to take an additional ten percent of your income. Say it was graduated but for you it was ten percent. And that would be given *just* to the war on poverty."

"I don't know," she said, "to be honest with you. To be honest with you, we're taxed an awful lot. It's amazing when you're a homeowner, and I think the state of

Wisconsin is high too. What did we figure? Oh golly, I forget how many thousands of dollars Bob makes that goes just for taxes right off. Whether we're willing to pay more?" She paused. "I'm not sure. I'd like to help people, but am I willing to pay more? No, probably not."

The conversation drifted to the Vietnam War. Mrs. Bertling said, "And then of course he [Kromholz] was spouting off about anti or draft dissenters, who to see about your draft card bit and all this, and I just sat there. I didn't believe in it then, I don't believe in it now. 'Course our church backs this, we're not for the Vietnam War. The church will help you evade, get out of the draft. If the church felt this way, if you could take a vote of all the people in the church, [and they said] yes, and I'd say well this is what they want. But it isn't.

"Palmer Freres is an officer in the American Legion and of course just hates to think anything like this, and then Bob was in the Korean War, an old veteran, they just don't like that kind of — If they've had to go over and fight — Bob didn't want to go over but we figured if he had to go, he had to go. The Korean War was a crazy war, up and down hills for no real reason, really dumb.

"Well, we did all this and it's not that I think every-one else has to do it, but I mean, is it a different kind of war for that reason? I mean, war is hell, it's bad all the time. How can it be any different? Someone tells you there's this war, we have to fight it, there's a reason. I wish there was an answer that we wouldn't have to fight. Then we go back to the old bit, there's a certain balance in nature. If it's not war, it's going to be this, famine."

And you just have to accept this?

"I think you do to a point. What do you do when someone's taking over? How much can you just let it go? And then again, I hope it's fought right, I hope we're not just extending it for bad reasons [referring to the recent Cambodia action]. I'm assuming that the President has all the right advice, that it has to be settled, and we will be pulling out and all that."

As I was leaving Jean Bertling said to me, "I don't think much. It used to bother me — and being inactive. When we first moved to Watertown I started doing more then, working with kids in Girl Scouts and Sunday School. Well, you know as you get older, you just don't have *time* to worry about the world. I get a big enough thrill just balancing the budget, going to the store with enough to buy something extra. I know I'm a frauhousewife but it's an awful lot of work with three and taking care of the house, and Bob."

Final Action

I

Bob Bertling had mentioned several names to me of members of their ad hoc committee "to see what could be done." Chuck Yeomans, the alderman who had formally moved that open housing be adopted in Watertown, was one of them. I spoke to Yeomans in the box factory his father had bought years ago. He showed me their main product, fine quality boxes for department stores, and then showed me the "glamour aspect" of the industry, folding boxes, something the Ira L. Henry Company is just beginning to explore.

Chuck Yeomans has lived in Watertown all his life except for three years during the Depression. He has gone to the Congregational Church since he was six years old, has taught Sunday School for over twenty years and has been an officer of the church for a number of years. Yeomans is in his fifties.

"I think at first that Reverend Kromholz's sermons were innocuous in that they didn't bring in politics too much or what he felt were local problems. But then, in the winter, in the spring of 1968 he started getting involved in a local situation as far as trying to organize pressure groups on what type of weapons the police were to have in the police department, and it was in regard to mob control and things like that, and he got involved in personalities with our Police Chief, and he got involved with our Mayor and both of them at the time happened to be members of our church. And after being involved in the City Hall in several confrontations, then in a couple of sermons he referred to local people, not by name but by position, and as I look back, my wife and I of course are pretty close, and she belongs to the Congregational Church, and she dislikes controversy, more than I do, so I didn't make any move in regards to the church and the pastor until — I just started staying away from Sunday morning sermon because I just couldn't take it."

I asked how they made him feel.

"Well," Chuck Yeomans said, "they made me feel very angry. Because he would refer continually to the local situation. I was on the City Council at the time, and he would refer to the Mayor, to the Police Chief and to the whole Police Department. 'Well,' he'd say, 'did you know that your Police Department has tear gas and scatter guns and all the latest weapons to control mobs and is ready to bring them out at a moment's notice?' He'd say this in the sermon."

What did Yeomans think of the Police Department buying this equipment?

"Well, I felt that it was perfectly all right. I voted for it whenever it came up because there were mobs at the time, let's say not large mobs but people that were out of control in Milwaukee and Madison, and Father Groppi was quite active at this time, and I felt that the Police Department should be prepared. So I would stay away from church.

"Well finally, after maybe a month or so of staying away my wife got quite concerned. She didn't want to take part in the service alone, and it was around March or April of '68 when she said to me that *she* was concerned about the type of sermons we were getting. And she was getting pretty upset, she just didn't know what was going to come of the whole church. I think that this meant that our church in the spring of 1968 was getting pretty well polarized in two camps.

"Well, what to do? I felt it was unhealthy for the church, it was getting split. I wasn't a member of the church board at that time but I did hear members say financially things weren't too good. That their contributions were off. Well, we had this polarization and church attendance was also falling off, drastically. So I said to Marge, 'I'm going to organize something here and see what we can do to correct the situation.'"

Had he attended the big meeting in November?

"I was certainly happy that I did not attend that meeting," Yeomans said. "I'm not very smart on these things, I think, but I certainly was intelligent enough to see that there was no fair representation — from the people that talked to me about the meeting ahead of time, that's where I gather it was a pretty one-sided affair. It was organized by people that were against the ministry. And it got to be a name-calling affair, from what I hear. In fact, I feel the minister probably had a longer tenure because of the reaction of people that heard about it and were there. They were disgusted with it.

"So I had I believe there were five. I called five members of the church. I talked to Mr. Garlid [the church moderator] and told him what we were doing, that we were meeting once a week to see what we could do about the situation. I think it started about two months before the final church meeting. Maybe three months. So we met weekly up here [his box factory near the outskirts of town]. The first thing we tried was to work through the church board and we couldn't get any place there. They would take no action.

"So then I was delegated to go over to see our association pastor in Brookfield, Albersworth, to see him and explain the situation to him and said that I was representing the committee and that we felt the church was going down hill, people were staying away from activities in the church, including the Sunday morning service. So, we waited a couple weeks after this and nothing happened. He said he would talk to the minister, but that's all he would do.

"So then, by that time our committee meetings, people knew something was going on. They weren't publicized because we felt — well, we wanted to keep it small and see what we could do. But, along about this time, after my visit with Reverend Albersworth, a couple of people *not* on the committee said that we've got to do something, your committee doesn't seem to get any place.

"So next step was, we found in the Constitution that, oh, for a church meeting by petition, I forget how many names you needed, but we did, we organized a petition. I don't even know how many names we got. To have a church meeting regarding the minister's relation with the congregation. I think we just felt we needed a petition and we were asked to by these outside members. This is the part that was difficult at the time for me, personally. The petition went through and was duly handed to the proper official, the moderator, and he brought it to the church board, and they set a meeting.

"So we had our committee meeting and we all agreed that in a meeting you had to have a motion to discuss. Well we ended up, the only motion the committee would agree on, there was no haggling about it, was to sever our relationship with our minister."

II

The mood and perceptions of those who supported Al Kromholz is clearly seen in Kathy Isaacson's journal:

April 4th, 1968 — tragedy — assassination of Dr. Martin Luther King

April 7th — memorial service for Dr. King.

Rumors begin about a petition for removal of the Rev. Kromholz

May 1 — Circle — Marge Yeomans and Ginny Guyer conspicuously absent. topic of discussion: religion and politics

May 3 — to dentist, Dr. Reinhard says he was asked to sign petition but refused

May 7 — asked Jean Bertling if there was a petition and she said, "No, there's no petition."

Mrs. Isaacson told me, "I got her [Jean Bertling] by herself and, 'Say, Jean, is there a petition going around about removing the minister?' She said, 'Oh no, there certainly wouldn't be anything like that. That would be a terrible thing to happen.' And there was one going around, and her husband was doing the circulating. This was shortly before the petition was made public."

Her journal continued:

May 11 — Junior Dance Club — get the feeling people are avoiding you?

meanwhile petition "to call a meeting to discuss the pastoral relation" with 110 signatures

May 16 — Peg Johannsen calls a meeting to try to iron out rampant rumors. Futile.

Kathy Isaacson said, "We talked to Yeomans, everybody else as though they were middle or left of the road, as though they were equally on our side as we were."

I asked if it seemed important to figure out how it was all happening. She said, "Not really. I think we got to feeling rather isolated. All you could do was realize how organized they were and not have any idea how we could oppose it. We really didn't have any idea what was going on."

Pat Becker, a long-time Watertown resident and a neighbor of Chuck Yeomans, said, "What it boiled down to was one third of those people were not giving a dime to the church but still two thirds of them I think were still contributing. There were still about a third of them who were still going to church and who were not too happy with Al. Well, there were some of those like Chuck who began to think that in order, as he said, to strengthen the church, he began to think the thing to do is, if Al wouldn't resign, was to force him out. And then this would bring everybody back and then they'd all be happy. But as John [her husband] said, 'But what about those who like Al? Then you'll have the same situation, you'll have them gone.' Well, it never occurred to him."

I asked if she knew when the petition started.

"No, I was kept in the dark. Chuck did come over here, he was nervous about it. I could tell it bothered him. He asked John what John thought and John said he didn't think it was a good idea. Anyway, he was already doing it. Why ask John? He asked John when it was too late. I said to him, what about all of these people who are for Alan? 'Course he never thought of them."

III

Not surprisingly, the clearest memories of the May 19 meeting were held by those who supported Alan Kromholz. Frank Isaacson said, "When I came into that meeting, I knew he was dead because I looked around and saw all these strangers and they were all old people."

Chuck Yeomans read the motion. This had been discussed previously at their small committee meeting. Yeomans said, "Well, nobody was very anxious to do it, and I said, well, if nobody else will do it, I will. I'm not anxious to, because in a small community, any community, a church altercation, human nature is to despise and to treat people on the other side — certain people are afflicted by this — they treat them pretty rough. Not physically but in their relationship. They don't speak to you, for instance. So I said I'd make the motion. I was very careful about it, because, well, it was self-evident."

Myrl Pauli, the church secretary, was impressed with the wording of the motion. "Chuck Yeomans it was that got up and said for the good of our church and *be-*

cause they felt that this was what the Lord wanted them to do, was preserve their church — amazing, it's just amazing — anyway, that they sever their relationship."

Silence.

"There wasn't any discussion. There was *absolutely* no discussion whatsoever. *None* whatsoever," Sydney McQuoid said. "Mrs. Pauli was right near and my parents were around and they kept looking at you, what's going on? And we were getting a little hope because, gosh, if there aren't gripes, what's this all for?"

Betty Ebert said, "It was the *oddest* meeting. As everybody and his brother had come out with these gripes at this other meeting *no*body came out with anything at this meeting. And all these people I'd never seen in my life came to vote. Everybody sat on their hands. 'Course we defenders aren't going to get up and say, 'We heard you don't like this.' I mean you're not going to put the thoughts into their heads. And we waited and waited and nobody said anything."

Bob Bertling was the only one to make a statement.

Mrs. Ebert recalled that he said the following, " 'We realize that the minister feels he's right, he's young and he's enthusiastic and all that, but there's some things we just don't like. For one thing, we hear all about the troubles of the world on the radio, in the newspaper, in the theatre, on the TV, and we don't need to come to church to hear some more about it.' And he said, 'We don't like that, we don't feel that's what the church is for, to have to hear about all the world's ills,' and he says, 'especially as we walk into the church we have to walk by a poster that says, Vote for McCarthy. We don't like mixing politics with religion. And as far as open housing and all that, we don't like that pushed down our throats. If we want to back it, okay, and if we don't, okay. We don't feel that the church has anything to do about that.' "

Bob Bertling's memory did not contradict Mrs. Ebert's account. He told me he said, "something about I don't have to come to church and be a captive audience for a bunch of garbage that some man can spew out of his mouth up on the pulpit or something, words to that effect. And I have to be a good Christian respecting my minister as a man of God and sit there and listen to this stuff, when it just makes me fume because I read all this crud in the papers, I hear what a bunch of rotten people we are, and how prejudiced we are, and that we're doing this wrong and that wrong, and just in general, I kinda let her go."

Jean Bertling told him that he said a lot more. That jerked his memory again. "Well, I said about McCarthy, I don't like to see McCarthy buttons and the church being used for campaign headquarters, and I don't like to see the kids being led down a path of, a primrose path."

Sydney McQuoid recalled that Bertling "was the only one that said anything. I don't remember exactly what he said but I remember that it upset me. Very much."

Betty Ebert recalled that her daughter spoke. "Mary B. got up and said, 'If we feel badly about his being such an activist and such a sympathizer with the Negro problem, we knew that before he came.' And somebody said, 'But we didn't know he liked them so darn much.'"

Myrl Pauli said, "Some people said that he hadn't visited the sick, and there was one woman in the church who had been widowed and he hadn't called on her since her husband had passed away. She did not say it, her mother said it. I believe the woman was there too. She didn't name names but most people knew who she was talking about because this had been hashed and hashed and hashed and hashed over the telephones and over bridge tables."

Had he visited her or not? I asked.

"Yes, he had," Mrs. Pauli said. "She works full time for one thing and is not at home in the daytime. But he had called on her in the evening and I had a record in my hand of all the calls he had made. A record was kept.

And so I got up and I said the calls *had* been made, and if anyone wanted to see this, I had kept the records and here they were. Nobody said boo to that."

Pat Becker was on the Diaconate and was in charge of shut-ins. She told me that at this meeting "Myrl Pauli tried to say was it because he was not making calls? She had the records there and Al had made I don't know how many hundreds of sick calls and calls on people within the parish itself. So they couldn't say he was neglecting them. See, this was one of the things they kept saying."

She didn't think he was neglecting them?

Pat Becker, her voice raised, said, "*No.* He was out of town a period of one or two weeks while he was doing this with Father Groppi. The rest of the time he came back in town and stayed there. And even when he was gone, we asked him on the Diaconate, and I asked him because all this was coming up, are there any people who are ill? He said three. He'd seen them. And none of them were seriously ill.

"Some people wouldn't let him in. Jack Hansel was sick and Al went to see him and he wouldn't let him in the door. Al said he couldn't see him but the man was very ill and someone should. So I brought him a gift and said it was from the congregation and he seemed real pleased. He let me in the door. But if you say this man isn't calling on people and they don't let him in — " She burst out laughing. "But anyway Al was concerned enough to say somebody should see this man. We'd ask Al about these pastoral duties and he always satisfied us. And as long as I served on the Diaconate, our board was never never in a quibble over what he was doing."

A few people spoke for Kromholz. According to Mrs. Ebert, Weir McQuoid said, " 'We have to make up our minds tonight, we have to take a side, we have to see if we want to go ahead with today's problems as they relate to the church or if we want to go to the fundamentalist and the formal type. We have to decide in our minds.' "

In general, Al Kromholz's supporters felt that they could not defend him. "I kept waiting for somebody to give a good legitimate gripe so that I could answer them," Mrs. Ebert said, "but nobody did. The gripes they gave were so — it wasn't anything you could really answer."

Frank Isaacson said, "There was no official discussion. I said at the meeting he was fired that I thought the purpose was to hear the evidence and then act on it and that so far all that had been was hearsay. There was no official complaint, and I thought the purpose of the meeting was to air these complaints. There were none.

"*They* knew. They knew why they were there and there was no — need — to say it. They don't say anything. They just nod at each other, like this, and they *know*. There's no need to say anything or actually make a decision. They just nod."

The discussion was over. The vote was to be held and the non-members of the church were asked to leave the room while the voting, by secret ballot, took place. At this point, for those supporting the minister, an almost surrealistic incident occurred. Sydney McQuoid said, "Then I heard this whole big ruckus out in the back and I didn't know what was going on and Dave Schultz came back after the vote and he said, 'Oh God, I got kicked out by the Mayor.' He said the Mayor came up and said, 'Get out of here, you damn little kids, who do you think you are?' and he pushed them out the door. Everybody was just flabbergasted. Dave came and snuck up in the front and told us about it and it just really upset me."

"And then they had the vote," Mrs. Ebert said. "And lo and behold, 133 to 77. And it was devastating. And of course, and oh gosh, this gal [Sydney McQuoid] and Myrl Pauli went into tears, I mean they just plain broke down. Myrl just couldn't believe it, or couldn't understand it, it just didn't make any sense to her. We had to pull Sydney away from him. She was just desolate. And then some of us went to McQuoid's after just to talk it over."

Sydney McQuoid recalled it also. "It was very tense. We knew what was going to happen but we were waiting for it to be said. Garlid said it. Then we all started crying. Kathy Smith, and Mrs. Pauli, and my mother, and Scott, and Jeanie, and me. Afterwards my parents had some close friends over. I didn't want to ride home, I just wanted to walk around by myself. Kathy was real upset too and we figured there was no use in us being together 'cause we'd just upset each other more. I went for a walk and I went over to Mark's [her boy friend] and I cried, and I cried at him, and screamed at him and yelled at him, and we walked around and he got me under control."

I asked how Al Kromholz reacted when it happened. "He hardly changed," Sydney said. "And he comforted us."

Myrl Pauli said, "The Congregational Church in this town is *the* church. If you want to be somebody when you come to this town, you join the Congregational Church. Sad but true. Effect on its politics? I think wealthy conservative people belong to it. I'm one of the throwbacks," she laughed. "We just grew up in the church and were confirmed. And so that it's the 'best church' couldn't mean beans to me.

"They want to just be a nice comfortable little social club. Our church. They talk about our church and their conception of what the church is is entirely different from what I think our church should be. They think it's a little building down on the corner of Fourth and Wisconsin, and it isn't. I mean that isn't what I want my church to be. But that's where they come to their meetings, and worship on Sunday, and sing in the choir. There is a majority that has no conception of what it means to reach out in this community.

"Our women's club doesn't even want to invite the Episcopal women over for an annual tea," Mrs. Pauli said. "And Mr. Shepard [a former minister] told me that there are people in this church who thought he was leading them down the road to Rome. You'd be surprised how much of this stuff there still is. They still hate the Catholics, so imagine how they feel toward black people. They say there is no prejudice in this town. Baloney.

"They're willing to send money and clothes, but when it comes to Milwaukee and tutoring, or helping in a Head Start program or something, this is something else again. They just don't have time to tear themselves away from their bridge games.

"I've lived in Watertown almost all my life except for a few years during World War II. Right, I grew up here. And I've always thought that Watertown is — pretty good. It's a good place to raise your children. It's not like a big city with all the hustle and the bustle and so on, and it's close enough to Milwaukee and to Madison if you want some real culture." Mrs. Pauli laughed.

"For ten years that church became so much a part of my life, and then it let me *down* so utterly, that I couldn't care less. For years, you didn't believe it was here until it finally rose and hit you over the head. Because when people said there is no prejudice here, you believed it, because there was never any confrontation."

When I asked the van der Hoogts if they had any problem deciding which way to vote, Van, who had voted to dismiss Kromholz, said, "I don't think so."

Pat van der Hoogt said, "We didn't go to the meeting. At least I didn't. I did not go. I could not — I felt that he was not the man, but I could not go and be the one to say — I could not vote him out. That sounds wishy washy but — I should have gone and voted him in but I did not feel he was good for the church. If I'm going to take a stand I couldn't have voted him out — because I didn't feel I was God to decide."

Frank van der Hoogt said, "Neither am I, nobody is saying that."

She said, "I'm not arguing with you. This is the way I felt inside."

"Look, this is ridiculous," Van said. "Take religion out of the whole picture. It's sort of like letting an employee go."

"But I don't think of a minister as my employee," Pat van der Hoogt said.

IV

I asked Alan Kromholz what he remembered of the meeting.

"I remember quite clearly I was fired," he said. He paused. "What do I remember of it? I suppose many things. I knew I was going to be fired before then. I mean, it was *fact*. So the firing came as no surprise. I told the conference officials the day before that I would be fired and that the vote would be two to one against me. The vote was 133 to 77 which certainly was pretty close to that two to one margin. Although I remember really preparing nothing for that meeting. Except to see that the participants were going to be there, that there was some structure. And probably the only demonic thing that I did was to make certain that as part of the order of the meeting for that evening the last hymn was 'Lord, We Thank Thee for Our Brothers.' That was *set*. Because I felt that it would be sort of hypocrisy and I don't know, as I look back on it now, I think it was joyous. The congregation stood and in one of the best congregational voices, in fact it was one of the loudest singings I had heard in the church, 'Lord, We Thank Thee for Our Brothers.'

"I remember quite clearly that initially, I think it was Bob Bertling took the thrust at the charges against me, that I didn't minister to the sick, and the dying, the bereaved. That I had been derelict in that. Although it took some time to pull that out and I recall Mrs. Pauli standing up and saying, 'Well, what are *the* specific charges?' rather than these, oh, shadowy phrases. And as Bertling tried to pin down that I had not called on the sick, I recall Myrl Pauli pointing out that there was on record every call that I had made."

I asked Kromholz if he thought they really believed the charge.

"Oh, I think it was an issue raised in *every* parish where the minister is charged with not doing his duty but getting involved in social activity."

Well, was there any ground for those charges?

"If I — how do I feel about them?" He paused. "I can't come up with the words to tell you how I feel about them. They were false charges, and sometimes it pains me a little that statistics weren't enough — to cram down the throats of these people.

"There were other charges. I recall one of the families who became violent opponents, let's not say violent, were uptight because they felt that at the time of bereavement they did not receive a ministry. I can't think of the last name. The man who died, Chub. Oh Alice, what was Alice's? I can't think of the family's last name right now. Part of that went back to the fact that while I had been there shortly after the death, like within the hour, spent time with the family, called several times on Alice after the death of her husband, anyway, one of the reasons they got turned off is on Sunday after the death, while flowers were on the altar, there was neither mention of the fact that the flowers were from the funeral nor was there mention in the bulletin of that fact, nor did the prayer specifically point to the family.

"And how do you defend against those kind of charges? Those are feelings and emotions. Perhaps laden with some guilt on the part of the family or people. Or the fact that death, whether they feel it or admit it, is the moment for them to take sort of the limelight of the community. And they just didn't get enough limelight."

What else happened at this meeting?

"Let's see. We talked about Bertling's charges and Mrs. Pauli's response to them which to me was very pleasing, at least that *someone* knew. It surprised me, as I recall it, that the Mayor did not speak. As I recall it. But perhaps that was because he knew what the outcome of the meeting was and there was no need for him to chance anything. I recall *after* that [meeting], a number of people saying, I just couldn't come. But they sent their condolences later on."

How did Ruth feel after it?

"I don't know. I believe — I would articulate her feelings as relief that it was over. Shocked by the congregation's action. Dismayed. Angry. And anxious to get out of town."

And how did you feel?

"Somewhat tense." He paused. "One, because I still lived within the community and therefore I have to live with the fact that I was fired. Aware of the fact that it had made some impact on my son, who was in school. Aware of the fact that I had to find a job and aware of the fact that the conference wasn't offering me any other church."

Was there some reason for that?

"I don't know. I never asked them that. Except basically to be told, there's no place to send a clergyman fired over social issues.

"I suppose in some respect I also felt proud. I had determined that I would not resign. I was asked five times basically to resign by various people in the church."

I asked why he wouldn't resign.

"Well," he said, "it was my feeling that the congregation, not a group of individuals, had hired me and had acted in a church service to install me, and to affirm that hiring. Therefore, really, they called me to the parish. And I felt that the issues were significant issues and therefore the congregation should take a stand on it and make it very clear cut. Why should I resign and move to another parish and get patted on the head as a nice pastor by the church? That's hypocrisy."

A number of people had made their feelings about Kromholz quite clear and I asked him if he could describe how he felt toward various people. I asked him to start with supporters and maybe not go any further than that. I mentioned Weir McQuoid's name.

"Well, let's take Mac." He paused again. "Mac was great. Mac was a supporter. Mac also was an individual that I could turn to for counsel and that I did turn to for counsel and who occasionally counseled slowing down, particularly I think with the young. I think Mac became very concerned, maybe even disturbed at the point when things were really blowing up."

You weren't?

"Yeah, I was concerned but I knew — there was no other way to go."

Why not?

"As far as I was concerned there was," the next was said very measuredly, "no — other — way — to — go.

"To listen, to dialogue, and to ask for a mature relationship, which I think I was trying to do from the congregation. This is what I got from Mac, I mean. This was a man. A man who I think was deeply religious, and one — well, okay, I loved Mac, all right?

"Harry Miller and Frank Isaacson are two people I would put on the same level with Mac. Harry Miller was superintendent of the church school. Harry worked hard at building the church and building good education programs. We had an excellent working relationship. No man in terms of working to get things done worked harder. There were many others."

How about Frank?

"Frank Isaacson. I would put him with Mac. He was a supporter. He could dialogue. He would talk, and he would go into the meetings to — argue — creatively. He bought nothing."

I said, You seem to be relating to people only in terms of support.

"Oh, I think that's how you phrased your question."

Because I interrupted him, Al Kromholz did not continue his discussion of those who supported him but went on to discuss his feelings about two people who had opposed him, one of whom, Mayor Bentzin, he spoke of with some anger. Later he said, "We should talk about one other thing. You asked me about people in the church. You never asked me about the community, of people in the community. There was a Father Thilman who was, and a Father Green, who were, as far as I'm concerned, my spiritual fathers. They ministered to me when *no* other clergymen in the community could do that. You know, when I was hurt. And were supportive, who listened to me and who were able to talk about strategy, and who were supportive in *many* ways beyond words. You gotta look at the Heinens, Burbachs, at so many people beyond our parish."

Kromholz named several more people, including Del Miller, minister of the sister United Church of Christ, who resigned under pressure shortly after Kromholz was fired.

"One thing I never said to the people in Watertown was how grateful, how deeply grateful I was that the fight was carried on after I left," Al Kromholz said. "Every man's revolution is a small one."

v

"Well," Frank Isaacson said, "I still feel that doing something, I think he [Kromholz] said this, doing something is better than doing nothing, even if you do something wrong. That's probably right. Although I'm not certain, but it's probably right.

"I'm sure Alan had decided that conditions were intolerable for some people and it was right that those people who had it so good should be willing to help those people who don't have it so good. And that the only way to get them to help would be to make them know that things weren't so good, and make them face these issues. In fact he told me that, he told me it was better for them to act and fire him than to sit there. Well, that's interesting. I'm not convinced that it is better. I mean, I'm not sure that we're any better off. It's hard to judge if he really helped us. He certainly tore it up and made people search their souls. There's no question about that. But as far, if his goal was to tear it up and make people search their souls, then he did it well, but if it was to convince them that society had to change, then I'm not sure.

"I think one of the key parts is understanding what is meant by a minister. What the role is. And I'm pretty well convinced that his idea of what is appropriate is quite different than mine. He sees it as ministering to the larger community, not to someone that hired him necessarily, and I have to admit I have trouble with that. He saw himself as an outgoing kind of minister to the larger community and not a minister serving a pastorate, as a closed unit. Not only that, he actually saw himself as prophet. He says so, his ministry is prophetic rather than pastoral. I think it helps explain what he did, his own rationalization for being able to go and march, or doing whatever, or working with *Soul* with the kids from all around, anybody, or working with the Human Relations Council or the Coffee House or whatever."

At the time was there any question about which side they would be on?

Kathy Isaacson said, "No, none at all."

Did they question his tactics then?

"No," Mrs. Isaacson said. "That was the beginning of confrontation politics and it all looked like it would work. It was being used by people all over the country and sometimes it was working. Especially with Martin Luther King's marches. The prospect of using it here as a tactic seemed like it stood a chance." She laughed. "It was one of the first failures of it.

"I think all during that time we couldn't figure out

what in the world everybody was so upset about. We could see no issue over whether to support open housing or not. It was just a matter of, 'of course.' No issue about whether to support McCarthy in a primary or not. No awareness that people wouldn't see these things as perfectly logical things to do.

"It's kind of shattering to see all these nice polite people — vicious. I can't think of anything anybody could have done differently."

Frank Isaacson said, "See, a lot of people read a lot into what Kromholz said from the pulpit that I really didn't see as bad and so I didn't realize the thing was boiling for a long time, because I thought these were things that probably should be said. I thought it was okay if these things were said, even though they're not pleasant. But the older people, not only did they think they were unpleasant but they weren't necessary at all. And they were getting really excited about it. They were having bridge club sessions of people who'd been together for years about how awful it was to go and listen to that stuff."

Do you think it really shook them up?

"I think it shook them very much, very seriously," Isaacson said.

Did they admit it to themselves?

"Yeah. Well, no. I don't know. They admitted it to the point that they saw that this was a problem that had to be dealt with. I think they probably feel they've solved it. I think that it really did shake them. For instance, [our] next-door neighbors had not been to church, I don't think, the rumor was they hadn't been to church since they were married. They're members and they donated some money. They came for the vote to oust him. Now that's a kind of fear that someone convinced them that it was very essential to get the right number of votes to that meeting."

The Isaacsons told me there were the real reasons and the pronounced reasons why Kromholz was fired. Mrs. Isaacson said the real reason was "for being a Communist."

Frank Isaacson said, "I think that he represented change, and it was okay to say he was Communist because that covers a lot of things. I think that he represented something different from them."

"It would have shattered everything that — their very way of life," Kathy Isaacson said. "Race prejudice played a part, I think. Just the thought of having all those colored people moving out here and those rumors of busloads of black people coming." She said the alleged reason was that "politics had no business in the church."

Speaking of alleged reasons, Frank Isaacson said, "The main reason was that he was not serving his pastorate. One of the jobs, one of the paramount jobs of the pastor is to call on sick people when they're in the hospital. I mean that's a commonly known fact. This *is* the way the pastor behaves. And if he does not, this is derelict. I mean, how could he call on people if he's in Milwaukee marching? That would be their remark."

Half a year after the firing Kathy Isaacson wrote the following letter to friends:

You would have to ask that nasty question, "What difference does it all make now?"

Would you mind terribly if I didn't even try to give a coherent answer to it? I mean, responses come to mind, and I try to separate, "but now that's a personal reaction, this is a problem reaction, etc." and I don't want to carefully outline this letter and then compose it. So I'll ramble on in my usual (but tonight somewhat less obscene) way. Also, I don't think the emotional impacts are so much less valid than the strictly sociological or political or task centered conflicts, in so far as they achieve an end result.

"Sociologically, it sure produced group cohesion or solidarity. Like we know who the we's are and who the they's are for sure. Like we really know it. And there don't seem to be enough we's.

She discussed certain interpersonal tensions in the community, the strange coincidence of the police car parked outside the last two Human Relations Council meetings, and the result of the national election.

Having the election over seems to relieve the emergency for the they's, though it doesn't make much sense. It must even be a little bewildering to them to see Nixon "cooperating with President Johnson in every way possible to achieve peace." Wallace got about 300 votes in Watertown. Less than I expected but just shocking to some people.

Frank is on the pastoral selection committee and I must reveal the committee experience with their first interview. They went to hear a Pastor Marshall in Delavan and met with him, then met a few days later. Lois Shannon, chairman, had received a letter from him and started to read: "Dear folks, (roughly transcribed) I wish to thank you for coming, you have helped me make a decision that has been bothering me for some time. I've decided to leave the church." He concluded with something like, "God may have to destroy the church and pick up the pieces in order to salvage anything."

Isn't that beautiful? Can't you just see that stunned righteous committee. Wow. "Hell those ministers are all alike. Can't trust anybody. We're surrounded by nuts."
So
the moon shines on the baseball diamond
there are human beings in the soup business
forty three forty three twelve percent
ratio symbolizing carbon monoxide
daisies coal mining birth toothpaste
wheels turn good times roll on goes the
legislative process
    but what is your relationship to me
are you real can we get into each other
with a mask or a straight face.
    Your question still unanswered after three pages,
I guess I haven't any answer.

Speaking of the aftermath of the conflict and the resulting polarization of the community Kathy Isaacson said, "I think in a sense though it would be nice to have a sense of community."

"For instance," Frank Isaacson said, "we were in a group of probably twenty, thirty people, a number of them from our church, and we used to go to a lot of cocktail parties, not that that's a particularly good thing, it was just one of the things that we did, and I'd say for awhile there once every two months, four times a year we'd be going to something, or somebody's house to a party. That's virtually stopped."

For you or just stopped?

"For us. No, it goes on. We dropped Junior Dance but I think we were cut before that."

Kathy Isaacson said, "People usually have cocktail parties before the dances and when we quit the dance club, where it would have been awkward not to invite us before, now they wouldn't have to worry about whether when we got to the dance that we weren't invited to their cocktail party."

"They think we're misguided," Isaacson said. "How can such a nice young professional man with such a nice home and pretty wife and beautiful kids be totally corrupted? He must be misguided."

"When it's an all-out assault," she said, "you can't get down to 'he's a nice guy.' It was a question of very basic values, very basic way of ordering your life. And then being a nice guy doesn't count."

What kind of values? I asked.

"Oh, equality of mankind," Kathy Isaacson said.

"But for them," Isaacson said, "the basic thing is keeping the status quo. Let's not change for change's sake. The question is: do you *really* believe people get a raw shake? They believe they get what they deserve."

VI

The G. Gordon Fraters are an older couple, genteel and respected. Fifteen years ago Gordon Frater turned G. B. Lewis Company from a business selling beehives totaling $400,000 in sales per year to a business producing industrial plastics at the sales rate of $6,500,000 per year.

We sat on their porch high above a large crook in the Rock River, above willow trees and a hill covered in lush lawn. The sun was setting golden on the river. It was very gracious, very lovely, very tranquil. Although he is retired, Gordon Frater wore a white shirt and tie. He has very slight white sideburns and is rather distinguished looking. Hazel Frater looks several years younger than her husband and was very slightly uneasy.

Gordon Frater said, "We really can't tell you that much about it for two reasons. One, we were not in the heart of the situation perhaps. And two, we've made up our minds that it's a closed matter."

Mrs. Frater said, "Some people dwell on it and become unhappy and begin to see faults where there were none. It happened, I'm sorry, and let's go on from there."

"The man himself was a very charming individual," Frater went on. "He had a tremendous amount of drive, something we in industry value very highly. In fact, I endeavored to help him. He talked to me quite freely. But he was too impulsive and consequently he tripped himself up. We never discussed any problem with anger or antagonism.

"You know of the interviews and publicity he gave out to the newspapers and over the radio. This sort of thing is definitely distasteful, completely unnecessary. And he used some of the church equipment and this was used against basic regulations of the church. In fact, my son offered to print it, if he could see it first, edit it. There were some peculiar things said at the time. Like that one girl had to withdraw from this newspaper because her father would lose his job. I know this is completely untrue as my son is his employer. And things like this were said at the time. I really don't care to discuss hearsay. We've heard many things but you can't trust it. It's just like reading the newspapers. I don't know if you agree with me on that, but it seems to me that our news media are terribly biased. Mr. Kromholz had many misconceptions of employee-manager relations. His drive would be widely sought by employers, if combined with lubrication. He had the aggressiveness, and I believe he could have had the lubrication."

"And he had charm," Mrs. Frater said. "Just in everyday talk, he was a very charming individual."

Frater added, "And yet he had such misinformation about human beings."

I asked why he had to be let go.

Frater replied, "His thinking was not acceptable. He was devoting entirely too much time to activities outside of Watertown. He was taking time away from his duties here. He held a meeting in the church that ended up quite strictly a political affair. Let's put it this way, on many subjects he completely failed to show both sides."

Mrs. Frater said, "He said he would call on everyone and this is not so important to us but I know of this one woman who asked for him to call on her and he came to her door and said, 'I have exactly fifteen minutes. What do you want?' Well, you know a minister just doesn't do this. It's not right."

"I don't think his interests were in the ministry," Frater said.

She went on with her train of thought. "And in some cases where someone died, he conducted the funeral and then didn't call afterwards. We have a great many older people in the church and he was young and I think this was part of the problem. And he didn't understand Watertown people at all. He had absolutely no understanding of Watertown people. You see, people here are mostly of German descent and have hearts of gold, but they can't be pushed."

Frater said, "It's funny for a Scotsman to say it, but I think the German are more stubborn than the Scotch. I think he felt the community was taking an anti-racial viewpoint. In that respect he was completely wrong."

I asked what they thought of the open housing bill in Watertown.

He replied, "Oh. Well, basically the thing's not needed. Why create a problem where it doesn't exist?"

Mrs. Frater said, "We were criticized and there

wasn't any problem. The Human Relations Council just created a mountain out of a molehill."

"He endeavored to secure employment here for Negroes," Frater said. "But he insisted that they be guaranteed a permanent job and at a specified wage. Now, this is impossible. A job can't be guaranteed. No employer can guarantee what he was asking. No, there was much he didn't know about industry."

"One thing always got me," Mrs. Frater said. "Sure we feel very sorry for the Negro, but how about the poor Indian?"

I asked what they saw as the role of the church.

"Spiritual guidance," she replied.

"And if they do that, the other problems take care of themselves," Frater said.

Should the church be involved in social action?

Frater said, "I've answered that. Not very deeply for sure."

Mrs. Frater said, "Ministers don't seem to understand our everyday selves. I don't know what I mean. I think that they're too idealistic. One time we were at the home of a lady recovering from an operation. Three of us went to visit her and Al came to visit her. She was a widow, and nearly blind and walked with two canes and somehow we started talking about possessions. He said we should be able to give away all our things, they're not important. She looked around. Her things were *all* she had. She looked at us and we wanted to bean him. But I'm sure he didn't know he had hurt her. And *ideally* I suppose he's right."

The conversation turned to more general topics. Frater criticized the news media for being too spectacular and cited *Life, Time,* and *Newsweek.* "There's so much just plain junk. So it's true. Who cares? If they would only glorify the man who does the common thing."

Frater said he thought *The Christian Science Monitor* was a good paper.

Mrs. Frater said, "There's so much to learn. We've got to learn we must always change."

Frater went on, "And there's always been a generation gap. When I was a kid, I couldn't whittle on Sundays because it broke the Sabbath."

What do they think of the poverty program?

"When they teach responsibility with help, wonderful. But until that time, it won't work," Mrs. Frater said. "With too many people it's gimme, gimme, gimme."

Frater said, "They must be helped to help themselves, not to just get."

I asked what they thought of Groppi.

Mrs. Frater said quietly, "That's the one question that could explode."

"It was misdirected, misguided activity," he said. "I don't think a great deal of rioting was connected with the marching but it aggravated people, stepping off the sidewalks to get around the marchers."

Mrs. Frater said, "I laughed. It was so ridiculous. It just seemed so ridiculous that people would waste their time doing that. I've heard so many people say, 'I was so firmly convinced we should do something but after these people threw themselves in front of cars, I'm so disgusted. It's done more harm than good.' I've heard many people say that."

Speaking of other ridiculous ideas Frater said, "Now in Vietnam, if we were to withdraw all our troops tomorrow, what would happen to the last fifty thousand? They'd be massacred just like at Dunkirk. It's just common sense and so it's just common sense to go into Cambodia and clean out some of the enemy weapons so they can't slaughter us. Give us a little more margin of safety when we withdraw.

"I know a fine Christian gentleman, not in this town, who's having church troubles. You know, with the minister. And he was telling me last week in my office that he's decided to withdraw all the contributions he's made to the church, and this troubles him very much as the church has always been important to him. He's going to withdraw all his contributions and even though it's not tax deductible, he's going to give it all to the Republican Party. 'It's our only hope, Gordon,' he said."

"I'm not sure I approve of that," Mrs. Frater said.

He replied, "Well, it's his decision and I respect it. It's something that people are being driven to such radical action.

"Now here's something I haven't seen in the newspapers at all but it was on TV. You know this hard hat march in St. Louis? Well, they showed them taking them off and using them on people. Now, this is better not shown. We see the results only and we don't know why they did it."

I said that there can be no excuse for violence like that.

"Oh yes, there can be," Gordon Frater replied. "We don't know how they were provoked. We don't know what provoked the shooting at Kent. *If* these guardsmen heard shots, *if*, and they were taunted and taunted —"

"How much should a policeman take?" Mrs. Frater asked. "There's a limit to what your makeup can take. That's a terrible thing. The whole thing. They say they shouldn't have loaded guns but what use would a policeman be if people knew the guns weren't loaded? None."

Frater said, "We appear to be taking the other side, but we don't accept what happened. I've been angry at cops on occasion." He told me a humorous story about a speeding ticket he had recently received. He said, "Like I said earlier, there's two sides to every issue."

DATE DUE
